W.A. & Ruby,

Merry Christmas!

2011

[illegible]

JESUS STORYTELLER

Timeless Truths from His PARABLES

DAVID O. DYKES

N COURAGE Resources

For a complete list of books and broadcast messages by Dr. David O. Dykes available in print, CD/Cassette or VHS/DVD, please visit the Discover Life online Resource Center at www.discoverlife.tv. Call toll-free 24 hours a day (888) 539-LIFE (5433).

Green Acres Baptist Church
1607 Troup Highway
Tyler, Texas 75701
www.gabc.org

Produced with the assistance of Fluency Organization, Inc. in Tyler, TX.

By David O. Dykes:

Revelation: God's Final Word

No, That's Not in the Bible

Finding Peace in Your Pain

ALSO BY DAVID O. DYKES:

Angels Really Do Exist: Signs of Heaven on Earth

Ten Requirements for America's Survival

Do Angels Really Exist?

Check for e-reader availability of books:

iPad kindle nook Reader

This book is dedicated to my buddy and first grandson, Grant David Holman.
I have faith that you will grow to be a faithful follower of Jesus, G-man!

Table of Contents

Introduction

I love a good story, don't you? I have a couple of good books going all the time because I've always loved to read. My favorite books are fiction—usually a mystery or thriller is all it takes to keep me turning the pages. As a boy, I remember reading under the covers at night with a flashlight so that my mother would not see the light still on in my room. Back then, I was really into the Hardy Boys mysteries and could not wait until the next day to find out how they were going to make it through another one of their harrowing adventures!

I guess that's why I like Jesus' parables so much. He was a master storyteller, captivating His audiences with humor, wisdom and insight into human behavior. He used simple, everyday objects and situations to explain God's truths in ways that everyone could understand. He talked about things like sheep in a pasture, a father and his sons, a long journey and a small coin. He pointed out the stories and truths hidden in our everyday world and revealed these timeless principles in unforgettable narratives that had a way of sticking with His audience long after He'd finished teaching. In fact, this was a key characteristic long predicted about the Messiah.

"His storytelling fulfilled the prophecy: I will open my mouth and tell stories; I will bring out into the open things hidden since the world's first day."
Matthew 13:35, *The Message*

As an author writing a book about someone as multi-dimensional as Jesus, there are countless angles I could take. His name is synonymous with so many things to so many people. For example, those who have trusted Him as Savior and Lord know Him as Jesus: The Forgiver. But He is also Jesus: The Healer. And He is Jesus: The Hope-Restorer. The Life-Giver. The list goes on and on. As a preacher-teacher, this book is about one of the many facets of Jesus I perhaps love the most—Jesus: the Storyteller. I hope you will enjoy reading it as much as I enjoyed writing it.

Pastor David
November 2011

CHAPTER 1
A Short Lesson in Studying Parables

Jesus' parables are some of the most well known stories in the world, including both secular and Christian audiences alike. He presented nearly one-third of His teachings as parables, scattered throughout the Gospels (the exception being the gospel of John, which does not contain any parables by the classic definition of the term). To be a student of what Jesus taught through stories, it's important to have a working definition of a parable. Our English word *parable* is a transliteration of the Greek word *para-bole*.

The word *para* means *alongside*. We have an English word *parallel* that carries the same meaning. We know a paralegal is someone who works alongside an attorney, and a para-church organization works alongside the church. The word *bole* literally means to "toss, or throw." Bowling, where one tosses a ball down a lane, comes from the Greek and Latin words, *bole*. So, a parable is something tossed or laid alongside something else. With that understanding, a good definition of a parable is: "A supernatural truth laid alongside a natural picture or story." Or, as it is popularly known, a parable is "An earthly story with a heavenly meaning."

Throughout His ministry, Jesus used miracles and parables as teachable moments to convey key truths. I believe there is a parable in every miracle and a miracle in every parable. When Jesus shared a parable or employed a metaphor, He used a picture, story or image that was easily understood by all. Alongside these simple stories, He laid down a powerful, life-changing truth. The story may have been basic, but the truths were deeply profound.

> A parable is "An earthly story with a heavenly meaning."

Beyond the classic parables Jesus told, He employed word pictures, analogies and metaphors throughout His ministry. In Matthew, for example, there are more than just the 15 stories that are traditionally considered parables. Therefore, when Jesus said, "You are the salt of the earth," He employed the basic principle of a parable. The literal topic of salt paralleled a spiritual truth. Christians are the moral agent that preserves society from impure influences. That's not a story, but it conveys an image that people can remember. (Which is a skill the best teachers use to reach their students.)

Sometimes Jesus specifically explained the spiritual meaning of a parable or word picture, but most of the time He simply laid down the natural truth, and His listeners had to ponder it and dig below the surface to discover the spiritual truth. Why did Jesus speak in parables instead of just speaking plainly? The disciples wondered the same thing. In Matthew, we read, "The disciples came to him and asked, 'Why do you speak to the people in parables?' He replied, 'The knowledge of the secrets of the kingdom of heaven has been given to you, but not to them. Whoever has will be given more, and he will have an abundance. Whoever does not have, even what he has will be taken from him. This is why I speak to them in parables'" (13:10-13).

Why did Jesus speak in parables instead of just speaking plainly?

I can't help but chuckle at the wisdom of Jesus because He answered their question about parables with a parable! To paraphrase, Jesus said that spiritual truth is so explosive that He didn't want to leave it lying around for anyone to grab. It's so valuable that if you want it, you're going to have to stretch to find it, but the reward will be worth the effort. To the one who finds truth, he or she will find MORE truth.

Jesus did not invent the use of parables in teaching. Parables were already a popular technique among Jewish rabbis for communicating truth. In fact, the Old Testament employed some powerful word pictures and even a parable or two. When the prophet Nathan rebuked King David for taking another man's wife, he told David a parable about someone who killed another man's prize lamb. The narrative was so convincing that the king initially thought it was a true story! The technique was extremely effective to get the king's attention and help him see the error of his ways. Isaiah also contains a parable about a man and the great pains he had taken to ensure he would have a bountiful harvest of grapes. He tilled the soil, cleared the stones and planted only the top-rated vines. However, when it was harvest time, the grapes were sour. This was a picture of the Jewish people who received everything from God, yet soured their relationship with Him.

Studying a parable of Jesus is similar to peeling an onion.

How to Study a Parable

Studying a parable of Jesus is similar to peeling an onion. Each story usually has several layers of application, which is another reason why the disciples asked Him to explain the meaning when He taught in parables.

OUTLINE OF A PARABLE:

Layer One: Plot of the Story

Layer Two: Historical Context

Layer Three: Personal Application

Let's look at an actual parable to explain how the idea of layered-truths works.

Layer One: The Plot of the Story

The outer layer of a parable is the story itself. For example, Jesus told the following story about two men who built their houses on different foundations.

> These words I speak to you are not incidental additions to your life, homeowner improvements to your standard of living. They are foundational words, words to build a life on. If you work these words into your life, you are like a smart carpenter who built his house on solid rock. Rain poured down, the river flooded, a tornado hit—but nothing moved that house. It was fixed to the rock. But if you just use my words in Bible studies and don't work them into your life, you are like a stupid carpenter who built his house on the sandy beach. When a storm rolled in and the waves came up, it collapsed like a house of cards. When Jesus concluded his address, the crowd burst into applause. They had never heard teaching like this. It was

> apparent that he was living everything he was saying—quite a contrast to their religion teachers! This was the best teaching they had ever heard. (***The Message,*** Matthew 7:24-29)

The story is so captivating, despite its simplicity, that the crowd claps! Their reaction speaks to the strength of Jesus' storytelling ability. This first layer of the parable, therefore, is the basic story itself.

This first layer of the parable is the basic story itself.

Layer Two: Historical Context

Below the surface layer of plot is the historical layer that spoke to Jesus' original audience. They knew exactly what He meant when He employed the imagery of a carpenter-builder, a home's foundation and the lethal potential of a storm. They'd seen the disastrous results for themselves many times. At other times, Jesus symbolized the Pharisees and Sadducees (the religious mafia, as I call them), and they knew exactly who they were in His stories.

For example, Jesus told a story about two men who entered the Temple to pray (Luke 18:9-14). One prayed a verbose prayer in praise of his own attributes in hopes he would gain favor with God and impress others. The other man prayed a humble prayer before

God, beating his chest and bowing his head. The peasants had to keep from darting their eyes toward the richly robed religious leaders listening in on Jesus' story. They knew which ones He was talking about—and the leaders no doubt knew as well!

Layer Three: Personal Application

The third layer is my favorite one because it answers the question, "So what?" If all Jesus did was tell nice stories and zingers that irritated the religious establishment, His teachings would not be as memorable. However, no one could escape the personal application of a parable. Why? Jesus knew from the onset what He wanted His listeners to pay attention to in the parable. He knew what truth we needed to hear and apply to our lives. Just because He couched it in a parable does not mean it is any less powerful. Sometimes, the storyline allows us to see ourselves in various roles and symbols imbedded in the plot. We're the prodigal son, or the pouting big brother who resents his homecoming. We're the lost lamb Jesus is looking for—or the man who finds the pearl of great price in the field. We're the crippled and lame guests of honor at the wedding feast, as well as the honored guests who gave all kinds of excuses not to attend. Sometimes

Below the surface layer of plot is the historical layer that spoke to Jesus' original audience.

we're the foolish builder, and sometimes we get it right and assume the role of the wise builder. That's the thing about the truths from parables—they're timeless. And no matter how many times we've read Jesus' parables, there is always something new for us to learn.

CHAPTER 2
What Is God Really Like?

The Parable of the Loving Father
Luke 15:11-24

Before the turn of the century, if you wanted to engage someone in a spiritual conversation, you steeled up your nerve and threw out a question like, "Do you believe in God?" The trouble is, I find that plenty of people are willing to say they believe in God these days. However, only when you press further do you discover it is usually a god of their own making. When I engage people in spiritual discussions today, I tend to reframe the question to be more specific. I'll ask, "What *kind* of God do you believe in?" Now, *that's* a question that will yield you a lot of information about a person's spiritual condition. There is something worse than being an atheist—believing in an erroneous concept of God. You can say you believe in God, but if you have a false idea of who He is, you are no better off than an atheist who doesn't believe at all. Better to have no clock at all than to rely on a broken one!

So, what is God really like? Some people say He is the same god of all the world's major religions, but He just goes by a different name. Is He the god of the Muslims? Is Allah just another name for the God of the Bible? Or is God more like the impersonal god of the Deists who think He started the world like a watchmaker winds a watch, but now He has grown tired of us, unwilling (or unable) to be involved in our lives? Hinduism, on the other hand, teaches us there are a number of gods and goddesses. Their greatest god, named Brahmin, is the all-pervasive life force inside every person. Is that who God is? Is He Allah? Or is He a watchmaker God? Or is He Brahmin? Or is He the good side of the Force in the Star Wars movies?

So, what is God really like?

Jesus Christ came to planet earth to show us exactly what God is like. It's not enough to believe in God; we must understand the nature of the God Jesus came to introduce.

In Luke 15, He shares three beautiful stories that paint an unmistakable portrait of the character and nature of God. Although the most well known one is often called the "Parable of the Prodigal Son" (you may even see that title inserted above the story in your Bible), the key figure in the parable is the Father. I prefer to call it the Parable of the Loving Father. Jesus is teaching us through this narrative that the God of the Universe is like the father in this story.

> There was once a man who had two sons. The younger said to his father, "Father, I want right now what's coming to me." So the father divided the property between them. It wasn't long before the younger son packed his bags and left for a distant country. There, undisciplined and dissipated, he wasted everything he had. After he had gone through all his money, there was a bad famine all through that country and he began to hurt. He signed on with a citizen there who assigned him to his fields to slop the pigs. He was so hungry he would have eaten the corncobs in the pig slop, but no one would give him any.

"...he ran out, embraced him, and kissed him."

> That brought him to his senses. He said, "All those farmhands working for my father sit down to three meals a day, and here I am starving to death. I'm going back to my father. I'll say to him, Father, I've sinned against God, I've sinned before you; I don't deserve to be called your son. Take me on as a hired hand." He got right up and went home to his father.
>
> When he was still a long way off, his father saw him. His heart pounding, he ran out, embraced him, and kissed him. The son started

his speech: "Father, I've sinned against God, I've sinned before you; I don't deserve to be called your son ever again."

But the father wasn't listening. He was calling to the servants, "Quick. Bring a clean set of clothes and dress him. Put the family ring on his finger and sandals on his feet. Then get a grain-fed heifer and roast it. We're going to feast! We're going to have a wonderful time! My son is here—given up for dead and now alive! Given up for lost and now found!" And they began to have a wonderful time. (***The Message,*** Luke 15:11-24)

> "My son is here—given up for dead and now alive!"

What God Regrets

According to Jewish law, a father who had two sons had to leave two-thirds of his estate to his older son and one-third to his younger son. In the story, the younger son made an unusual demand. He wanted to receive his inheritance although his father was still alive. This younger son came to his dad one day and said, "I know you're gonna' drop dead someday, but I don't want to wait—give me my money now." Of course, the son wounded the father with this harsh demand, but he granted it nonetheless. The Bible doesn't say, but he probably had to liquidate some of his assets by selling some land or livestock to come up with the money. Cash in hand, the youngest boy then walks out of his father's life and heads for the "far country." That night was the first of several nights the heartbroken father wept many tears over his son's foolish behavior. But the son? He didn't shed one tear. Not yet anyway.

In every parable, there are symbols and characters that represent spiritual truths. This is how Jesus communicated to His audience. It wasn't difficult for the original audience hearing this parable for the first time to recognize the father in this parable as God. He is a loving Father who will let you walk away from fellowship with Him, if you desire, even if it breaks His own heart to allow it. Some say the prodigal son represents a person who has never been saved. However, even believers can feel a tug toward the "far country" sometimes. When the son in this story left his father, he did not cease to be his son. The relationship remained intact, but the fellowship was severely damaged by his actions.

> **...He deeply regrets our rebellious behavior.**

That is one of the foundational qualities of God's loving nature that this parable helps us to understand at the onset. If you are a Christian, you cannot sever your *relationship* with God as His child, but you can certainly break *fellowship* with Him. And the strange truth is that God allows us to break it—although He deeply regrets our rebellious behavior. Once you become a Christian, God establishes a permanent love relationship with you. He is your Father and nothing can ever change that. He will never leave you, but if you choose to interrupt your fellowship with Him by disobeying, He loves you enough to let you go.

Free to Go

The God of the Universe has given a precious gift to humanity—the gift of free will. That means He loves us enough to let us exercise choice when it comes to loving Him or rejecting Him. What kind of relationship would we have if God made us love Him like a robot or puppet on a string? Instead, God says to each man and woman, "I love you, so you are free to go." God loves you so much that He will never force you to stay in fellowship with Him. If you are determined to do something as foolish as walking out on God, He won't stop you. He doesn't coerce obedience and loyalty from anyone; He wants you to freely love and serve Him.

> "I love you, so you are free to go."

I once knew a man who broke his fellowship with God because of disobedience. He became bitter towards God and asked me, "If what I did was so wrong (and it was wrong), why didn't God stop it?" It was almost as if he was blaming God for letting him mess up. Doesn't God have all the power? Couldn't

He have shot a lightning bolt down from heaven and short-circuited his sinful plans? God could have—but He didn't. Why not?

God didn't stop that guy from making the wrong choice for the same reason He didn't stop Adam and Eve from eating the forbidden fruit in the Garden of Eden. God didn't stop it for the same reason the father in this parable didn't fling himself across the door and say, "I won't let you leave!" That's one thing Jesus wanted us to know about the nature of God. He loves you so much that He allows you to make you own choices, even though He knows what the consequences will be. That's what true love does—to force us to stay close to His heart would not be love at all.

> **He loves you so much that He allows you to make your own choices...**

Parents of prodigals know exactly how the father in this story felt. Those of you with prodigal children or grandchildren in your family know the kind of pain God feels when His children walk away. For a time, you can discipline a wayward child. When they are too old for punishment to do any good, all you can do is feel the pain. Unlike God, we are helpless to do anything about it when a prodigal child breaks our hearts. God, who has all the power in the Universe, relinquishes that power to let prodigals have their way. So His pain is even greater because the greater the capacity to love, the greater the capacity to be hurt.

A Twist in the Plot

In our parable, the wayward son didn't fare so well in the far country. He lived high on the hog for a while, but pretty soon he was low *with* the hogs! Jesus uses six words in verse 13 to describe what happened: He "squandered his wealth in wild living" (according to the New International Version, abbreviated "NIV"). With a pocketful of money, he headed straight for the casinos and strip joints and soon blew all of his funds. Before he could turn around, it was all gone. Penniless and without a friend in sight, he ended up in a pigpen slopping hogs. Jesus said he "came to his senses" when he realized a servant in his father's house had it better than he did. All of his father's farmhands got three meals a day, and he couldn't even eat the corncobs that the pigs were eating! He finally reached his P.O.T.D.—the Point of Total Desperation. So, he swallowed something more tasteless than corncobs—his pride—and started the long journey back home.

He finally reached his P.O.T.D.

Scholars have discovered a similar story to this one existed among Jewish rabbis for many years before

Jesus told His parable. In the earlier form, the younger son also ran away and spent all his father's money. However, what happened next is very different from what happened in Jesus' version. When the son came crawling home, the father rejected him! I imagine that as Jesus was telling this story, the Pharisees and tax collectors were nodding their heads and thinking, "Yeah, I've heard this one before." At this point in the story, they expected Him to say, "One day the father saw his son returning. He waited with his arms crossed. The broken-down son begged his father to take him back. That's when the father looked away from him in disgust and said, 'Forget it! You had your chance. You've chosen to live like a pig, now go back to your pigs. You've made your bed, now lie in it!'"

The broken-down son begged his father to take him back.

In the rabbis' story, the son got exactly what he deserved, which reflected the Old Testament idea of strict legalism. In fact, the Old Testament prescribed that a father could have a rebellious son stoned to death. Deuteronomy 21:18-21 says, "If a man has a stubborn and rebellious son who does not obey...his father and mother shall bring him to the elders and say, 'This son of ours is stubborn and rebellious. He will not obey us. He is a profligate and a drunkard.'

Then all the men shall stone him to death." That was the way the Pharisees expected the father in the Jewish rabbi version of the story to treat his son. However, Jesus has a surprise twist to the plot.

When God Runs

In Jesus' version, the devastated father thought of his son every day and wondered where he was and what he was doing. We can surmise that it's no coincidence that the father just so happened to see his son walking down the road one day. No, I imagine that each afternoon about sundown the father would walk to the edge of his property, stand at his stone fence and look down the road that had taken his son away. He was looking, longing, hoping that one day his son would return.

> Then he did an amazing thing.

On one of these afternoons, he saw a bent over figure dragging along the road. That couldn't be his son, he told himself, because his son always had a spring in his step and held his head high. Besides, this character was dressed in rags. His son always dressed in fine clothing. Even so, there was something about the disheveled figure that looked oddly familiar. In a flash, the father realized it *was* his son. Then he did an amazing thing. He jumped the stone fence and sprinted out to meet him. The Bible says, "While he was still a long way off, his father saw him and was filled with compassion for him; he ran to his son, threw his arms around him and kissed him" (NIV). The Greek verb for "kissed" indicates that he "kept on kissing" him over and over, smothering his son with affection.

In the Jewish culture, men wore long robes. In order for a man to run, he had to lift up the hem and hold it high to keep from tripping over it. In doing so, he would bare his legs, which was considered highly undignified. Men of respect *never* ran for any reason. Can't you see this respectable man grabbing fistfuls of robe, running toward his son? He didn't wait for the son to reach him; he *ran*. Remember, the son had been working knee-deep in a pigpen. He looked and smelled awful, not exactly the kind of person you want to hug and kiss! The father could have insisted he clean up first—instead, he accepted him just as he was.

...he ran.

At this point, the rabbis' storyline goes out the window. Jesus is showing his listeners a revolutionary portrayal of God. Jesus said God *runs* to meet us when we decide to return to Him. In fact, whenever we decide to head home after a season of being away from God, He meets us more than halfway. Some people have trouble with this plot twist. They are more comfortable with the original plot where God refuses to accept him back. They see God as a mean ogre sitting on a mysterious throne watching and waiting for someone to make a mistake so He can stand up and say, "Gotcha!" However, that's not the God Jesus described. Instead, He is a loving, compassionate God who deeply cares about His children, no matter how many times they have hurt Him.

> "There was no anger in his heart toward his son."

British pastor, Charles Spurgeon, described the scene this way: "It was not with icy eyes that the father looked on his returning son. Love filled his heart as he beheld him. There was no anger in his heart toward his son. It was true that it was all his own fault, but that did not come before his father's mind. It was the state that he was in, his poverty, his degradation, that pale face of his so wan with hunger that touched his father to the quick. We read that the father ran! The compassion of God is followed by swift movements. He is slow to anger, but He is quick to bless. God comes flying in the greatness of His compassion to help every poor soul that returns to Him." Despite what you may have heard about God and despite how an earthly father might react, that's what God is really like.

Back Where You Belong

Back in the pigpen, the son realized he had a lot of explaining to do. He started rehearsing a groveling speech he was going to give his dad to make up for what he'd done to him. His speech had three basic parts to it, but only two of his statements were correct. He said to his father, "I have sinned against heaven." That was right. All sin is primarily against God, so he was correct to confess his wrongdoing to God. Next, he confessed to his father because he knew he had sinned against him personally. Right again. One of the hardest things for any of us to say is, "I was wrong. Will you forgive me?" However, the next thing he said was off-track. He said with a heavy heart, "I am no longer worthy to be called your son."

After he left, he didn't think he deserved to be a son...

As good as that sounded to his shamed conscience, he had it all wrong. He was never worthy to be called a son of his father in the first place. He didn't earn his way into his father's prestigious family—he was born into it. After he left, he didn't think he deserved to be a son, so he was ready to ask his father to just make him like one of his servants. However, he had not earned his status in the family so how could he lose it? It was all by grace! No one is "worthy" to be called a child of God—it is all by grace that we are reborn into God's family.

Therefore, the father refused to entertain the idea that his son would be a servant. Remember, the relationship was intact—it was the *fellowship* that was broken. As a symbol of reconnecting that once broken fellowship, the father lovingly restored everything the son had lost in the way he dressed his son! Immediately the father commanded his servants to bring the best robe, covering all the filth and dirt of his mistakes. That's a lovely picture of how God covers our sin with a "robe of righteousness" (Isaiah 61:10). Sons also often wore a ring with the family seal engraved upon it, which they used to stamp in wax denoting their signature on important documents. My guess is that the son probably left with one of the family rings on his finger, but he had long since pawned it for money. The father put a new ring on his finger symbolizing his fully restored status in the family. Slaves didn't wear shoes, but sons did. So the father had sandals put on his son's tired, mud-caked feet. The old Negro spiritual "All God's Chillun Got Shoes" was based on this verse. Everything the son left in search of, he found back at his father's

...it is all by grace that we are reborn into God's family.

house—and more. His father's love for his wayward son had never changed. However, the son came back a changed man and would forever carry the scars and the regrets of his sinful behavior.

Now it was time to party. The father commanded the fattened calf to be killed so they could have a real Texas barbecue! The fact that the father had been fattening up the calf makes me think he anticipated the return of his son in faith. He knew he would treat him as if he never left—if only he would return. In the same way, when we return to our heavenly Father, it is as if we never left. He does not hold our sins over our heads, recounting all our mistakes before He welcomes us home again. He extends His arms of grace to restore us back to full fellowship with Him.

...when we return to our heavenly Father it is as if we never left.

For Families of Prodigals

In his book, *Capital of the World,* Ernest Hemingway wrote about a father in Spain who had a son named Paco. Because of his son's rebellion, Paco and his father were estranged. The father was bitter and angry with his son and kicked him out of the home. After years of bitterness, the father's anger finally ebbed and he realized his mistake. He began to look for Paco, with no results. Finally, in desperation, the father placed an ad in the Madrid newspaper. The ad read:

PACO, ALL IS FORGIVEN.
MEET ME AT THE NEWSPAPER OFFICE
AT 9AM TOMORROW.
LOVE, YOUR FATHER

Paco is a rather common name in Spain, and in his story Hemingway describes the father arriving the next morning at the newspaper to find 600 young men—all named Paco—waiting and hoping to receive the forgiveness of their fathers.

God understands your pain.

If there is anything our fractured families need today, it is a healthy dose of repentance and forgiveness between parents and prodigals. Your child (or grandchild) may be distant from you because of rebellion, a disagreement, a sinful lifestyle, a bad relationship, or any number of reasons why they may have walked out of your life. Whatever the reason, the pain of being out of fellowship with a child or grandchild is one of the heaviest burdens of a parent's heart. If you are in that situation, I want you to know:

(1) **God understands your pain.** Sometimes you

may want to croon a line from the old song that says, "Nobody knows the trouble I've seen." But that's not true, because God knows and He cares. He is the suffering father in this parable waiting every day for a child to return home.

(2) **Don't jump in the pigpen to rescue them.** In this parable, the father didn't go to the pigpen and try to pull his son out. That would have been tragic for both of them. The son had to realize his own mistake, in his own time. God used the filth of the pigpen to bring him to that realization. Some of you have kids in the pigpen right now and it's all you can do not to run in after them and rescue them. They must come to their own Point of Total Desperation before they seek God. If you circumvent that process, you risk losing the child forever.

Let the prodigal know the door is open.

(3) **Let the prodigal know the door is open.** Resist the urge to slam the door in anger or tell your child he or she is never welcome back into your home. Let them know you'll leave the light on for them whenever they are ready to repent.

(4) **Receive them when they repent.** True fellowship

> can never be restored until a prodigal child has repented. Notice that the son returned with a changed heart. The boy who left was not the man who came back home. A prodigal may return when he or she runs out of money and self-sufficiency, but if they don't repent, the problem is not resolved. It's only aggravated.

What a wonderful picture this parable paints of what God is like. He is a God who regrets your rebellion, runs when you return and restores you when you repent. For those listening that day, the message was a divisive one. Some were Pharisees who thought they were sinless—they didn't see a need for forgiveness, so the story was lost on them. However, there were tax collectors and others there who had fresh mud from the "far country" still on their feet. In this simple but surprising story, Jesus showed them the kind of God they needed most (yet never dared to believe was real). He painted grace with a face in his portrayal of a father's unrelenting love for his son.

> **The good news is that Jesus does receive sinners.**

Years ago, there was a bag lady in New York City who attended a preaching service at a Manhattan Rescue Mission. Afterwards in the line to receive soup, she mentioned to the preacher she was now ready to give her life to Jesus. She said, "I never knew until today that my name is in the Bible." The preacher smiled and said, "What's your name?" She said, "My name is Edith. And my name is in the Bible." The preacher said, "I'm sorry ma'am, but you must be mistaken. The name Edith never appears in the Bible." She said, "Oh yes it does...you read it a few minutes ago!" He opened his Bible and she pointed her dirty finger to Luke 15:2, where the setting of our story begins. "Read it out loud," she begged. The preacher read aloud his King James Version that says, "This man [Jesus] receiveth sinners and *eateth* with them." She smiled and said, "There it is! Jesus receiveth sinners and *Edith* with them!" And indeed, the good news is that Jesus does receive sinners—and Edith, and David, and you and anyone else who comes to Him. *That* is what God is really like.

That is what God is really like.

QUESTIONS TO THINK ABOUT

What did you think God was like when you were a kid? How did He look to you?

How can one's earthly father affect one's understanding of the heavenly Father?

Why does God give us free will—even if that means we reject His love?

What is tough love, and how did the father in this story express it?

In what ways do you relate to the prodigal in this story? To the father?

How is it possible to grow closer to God after a season of waywardness?

What are you learning about how to minister to prodigals?

CHAPTER 3
A Fool's Formula for Failure

The Parable of the Rich Fool
Luke 12:13-21

Each year, *Forbes Magazine* publishes its much-anticipated list of the ten richest people in America. Americans look at people like Warren Buffet, Bill Gates and Steve Jobs as the template for true American success. Wouldn't it be great if *Forbes* also published a list of the Ten Best Dads or the Ten Best Moms? How about the Ten Happiest Married Couples? I guarantee there would be little cross-referencing between the lists of the most successful and the most contented people in America today. In our culture, success is measured by how much money you make, how many toys you have and how much real estate or business interest you possess—regardless of the condition of your family and personal life.

One day, Jesus was in the middle of teaching on hypocrisy when He was interrupted by a couple of brothers who had a family controversy about how their inheritance was going to be divided. Apparently, while Jesus was speaking, all these two guys could think about was how much money each of them was going to get from their father's estate.

Instead of answering directly, Jesus once again cut to the heart of the issue with a parable about greed.

Jesus once again cut to the heart of the issue with a parable about greed.

> Someone out of the crowd said, "Teacher, order my brother to give me a fair share of the family inheritance." He replied, "Mister, what makes you think it's any of my business to be a judge or mediator for you?"
>
> Speaking to the people, he went on, "Take care! Protect yourself against the least bit of greed. Life is not defined by what you have, even when you have a lot."
>
> Then he told them this story: The farm of a certain rich man produced a terrific crop. He talked to himself: "What can I do? My barn isn't big enough for this harvest." Then he said, "Here's what I'll do: I'll tear down my barns and build bigger ones. Then I'll gather in all my grain and goods, and I'll say to myself, 'Self, you've done well! You've got it made and can now retire. Take it easy and have the time of your life!'"
>
> Just then God showed up and said, "Fool! Tonight you die. And your

barnful of goods—who gets it?" That's what happens when you fill your barn with Self and not with God. (***The Message,*** Luke 12:13-21)

There is one word in Jesus' story that rivets my attention: "Fool." Jesus warned in Matthew 5:22, "Anyone who says, 'you fool!' will be in danger of the fire of hell." Yet notice it is *God* who does the name-calling here. It doesn't bother me too much if another person insults me. Like Paul, I don't mind being known as a fool for Christ's sake (1 Corinthians 4:10). But I certainly don't want to reach the end of my life and *God* call me a fool. What kind of person and behavior warrants that title? Although the farmer appears to have made a good living, he is a total failure in life.

I certainly don't want to reach the end of my life and *God* call me a fool.

What Defines Success?

In Jesus' time, the economy was agriculturally based. This man was rich because he had a bumper crop with such a surplus that he had to build bigger barns! If that guy were around today, he would have created a genetically engineered, pest-resistant crop that could potentially feed the entire world. He would be considered a brilliant billionaire entrepreneur and named Businessman of the Year. However, God called him something else.

Like the foolish farmer, most Americans think they've arrived when they have accumulated so much stuff that they can just sit back and say, "Take it easy! Eat, drink, and be merry!" My friend, Steve Farrar, has re-written a Common Prayer that captures our cultural obsession with accumulating stuff:

Misery is no respecter of persons or net worth.

Now I lay me down to sleep,
I pray my Cuisinart to keep.
I pray my stocks are on the rise,
And that my analyst is wise.

That all the wine I sip is white,
And that my hot tub's watertight.
That racquetball won't get too tough,
That all my sushi's fresh enough.

I pray my cellular phone still works,
That my career won't lose its perks.
My microwave won't radiate,
And my condo won't depreciate.

I pray my health club doesn't close
And that my money market grows.
If I go broke before I wake,
I pray my Lexus they won't take!

(Steve Farrar, *Survival in the American Jungle*)

You've heard the expression, "Money can't buy happiness." Someone once commented that at least it lets you choose your misery. Not so. I've known wealthy people who were miserable—and poor folks who were just as unhappy. Misery is no respecter of persons or net worth. And death, which is the subject of this parable, is the ultimate equalizer among us—no matter how much money is in the bank. I once saw a t-shirt that read: "The one who dies with the most toys wins." However, someone much wiser revised that message to say, "The one who dies with the most toys—still dies!" And that's the truth that the farmer in this parable discovered one night.

> **And death... is the ultimate equalizer among us.**

The Gimme Generation

I once read that before September 11 Americans were known as the "Me generation," but since that terrible day we have become the "Us generation." I hope that's true, but I haven't seen much evidence of it, have you? I'd say we are more like the "Gimme generation." Gimme. Gimme. Gimme. Notice how many times the farmer used a form of the first personal pronoun in this story. He said to himself: "What can **I** do? **MY** barn isn't big enough for this harvest...Here's what **I'LL** do. **I'LL** tear down **MY** barns and build bigger ones. Then **I'LL** gather in all **MY** grain and goods, and **I'LL** say to **MYSELF, SELF** you've done well!"

Every fourth word was about *himself* (and a person who is all wrapped up in himself makes a pretty small package!). The essence of *all* sin is self-centeredness. Adam and Eve didn't eat the forbidden fruit in the Garden of Eden because they hated God; they did it out of selfishness. To satisfy their craving for the one taste they had not experienced, they ate themselves out of house and home! God evicted them from the Garden forever.

"He who trusts in himself is a fool."

Proverbs 28:26 says, "He who trusts in himself is a fool." And yet we're taught from a young age to look out for number one (or no one else will). The irony is that by focusing on pleasing yourself, you guarantee your own misery. The best way to have an unhappy marriage is by focusing on only your needs, rather than the desires of your mate.

A millisecond after the foolish farmer died, he discovered that he was *not* the captain of his soul. Jesus taught about losing your life in order to find it. William Carey, called the father of modern missions, was one of the first Baptists to take the Gospel to a foreign land. For over 60 years, he selflessly preached and taught the Bible in India. Before he died, he asked that these last words be engraved on his tombstone:

A guilty, weak, and helpless worm,
On Thy kind arms I fall;
Be Thou my strength and righteousness.
My Jesus and my all.

A self-effacing attitude like Carey's has no place in a Fortune 500 company. The runners of the rat race prefer the kind of hard-charging, go-getter who says, "I am the master of my fate." Did Carey live a successful life? Today, there are three universities named after William Carey. How many will be named after Bernie Madoff? When God passes out His rewards in heaven, His list won't be the same as *Forbes* or *People* magazine's Most Beautiful People. He will honor the William Careys of this world and thousands of others we don't even know because they lived their lives flying beneath the radar of worldly success.

Jesus taught about losing your life in order to find it.

If I Just Had a Little More Money...

The Romans had a proverb: "Money is like seawater. The more you drink, the thirstier you become." The farmer in this story assumed he had it made because he had plenty of goods stored up for many years to come. Howard Hughes made more than a billion dollars in his lifetime (back when a billion dollars was really a billion dollars!). However, he lived out the last lonely years of his existence as a recluse in the Xanadu Hotel in the Bahamas. Many had assumed his fortune would allow him to grow old eating, drinking and being merry. However, life did not turn out that way for Howard. His billions were no guarantee of a stress-free life—in fact, money only added to his trouble.

"Money is like seawater. The more you drink, the thirstier you become."

Like most Americans, you might think that creating more margin in your monthly budget would remove some major stress in your life. It might—for a while. Inevitably, however, more money can lead to even more negative returns. In fact, if you asked most wealthy people if having a lot of money reduces stress, you'd be surprised to learn wealth produces its own kind of stress and pressure. Great wealth is often more of a burden than a blessing.

Remember Solomon, the richest man in the Bible? In today's dollars, he would have been far wealthier than Bill Gates. However, as Solomon approached old age he wrote in Ecclesiastes 2:10-11: "I denied myself nothing my eyes desired ... my heart took delight in all my work, and this was the reward for all my labor. Yet when I surveyed all that my hands had done and what I had toiled to achieve, everything was meaningless, a chasing after the wind; nothing was gained under the sun." We can chase the wind, but we'll never grasp it. You can seek for happiness in the accumulation of wealth and possessions, but you won't find it. Jesus assures us that life on earth will *never* be trouble-free. The only stress-free people are in the cemetery! Job said, "Man is born for trouble as surely as sparks fly upward" (Job 5:7).

> "Man is born for trouble as surely as sparks fly upward."

Game Over

The farmer in Jesus' story understood the agriculture futures market, planting and harvesting, but he made one terrible miscalculation: he didn't count on dying so soon. There's a saying: "A fool and his money are soon parted." (Some say a fool and his money are some party!) But when the party's over, it's over. The fool and his money are separated—permanently. When people try to live as if there's no tomorrow, they really live as if there is no eternity. Compared to eternity, this life is incredibly brief. James 4:14 asks, "What is your life? You are a mist that appears for a little while and then vanishes." That's how long your life is from heaven's perspective! This parable proves there is another thing besides happiness that money can't buy—more time.

Jim Croce was a talented singer and songwriter who wrote and sang, "Time in a Bottle" about his desire to save time in a bottle in order to spend it later with someone he loved. By the time he released what would turn out to be a very popular song, Jim Croce was dead. Game over, you're out of time. Do we exist just to work 60 hours a week, so we can make a bunch of money, so we can retire and relax? From Croce's perspective, knowing that God can demand your life at any time changes your entire outlook. Suddenly, making as much money as humanly possible doesn't seem as important. So, what takes the place of the pursuit of more money and success? Jesus gives us a hint when He wraps up His story.

> **Compared to eternity, this life is incredibly brief.**

Toward the end of the story, Jesus resumes the role of a narrator. It's obvious that the farmer made the wrong choice—most of His audience got that one. Then Jesus adds something kind of mysterious at the end that must have made His listeners scratch their heads. Almost as an afterthought, He indicates there is another kind of wealth that has nothing to do with one's financial net worth. In other words, there's something worse than hoarding. Stockpiling his possessions was not the most foolish thing the man did—it was his total neglect of the greater opportunity to be rich beyond his wildest dreams. In the NIV translation, Jesus called it being "rich toward God." *The Message* paraphrase puts it in the context of the story and calls it filling your "barns" with God. How do you do that? No doubt, Jesus confirmed the truth that you can't take it with you when you die... but what if you could send it on ahead?

The Best Return on an Investment

Jesus confirmed the truth that you can't take it with you when you die...

George Washington Truett was the pastor of First Baptist Church in Dallas for 47 years (1897-1944). He once visited a wealthy West Texas rancher to have dinner in his palatial home. After a sumptuous meal, the rancher took Dr. Truett to a veranda on top of his house. He squeezed a big cigar between his teeth and pointed his finger toward a beautiful manmade lake in the south. "Preacher," he said, "I own everything in that direction, as far as you can see." Then he pointed east toward some cotton fields and said, "And I own everything in that direction, too." Next, he took a big puff on his cigar, pointed north toward a huge herd of cattle and bragged, "And I own everything as far as you can see in that direction." Turning toward the setting sun, he said, "And I own everything you can see in that direction." "Except the sun, of course," he added in mock humiliation. Dr. Truett turned to his host, pointed straight up to the sky and said, "And how much do you own in that direction?"

Someone can be dirt poor financially and still be the richest person on earth—if he or she is "rich toward God." In God's economy, both a vagabond and a millionaire may be equally rich toward God. It all depends on the *location* of their treasure. Most real estate experts will say the three most important factors in real estate are: location, location, location. The same is true with your riches: location, location, location. In Matthew 6:19 Jesus said, "Don't hoard treasure down here where it gets eaten by moths and corroded by rust or—worse!—stolen by burglars. Stockpile treasure in heaven, where it's safe from moth, rust, and burglars. The place where your treasure is, is the place you will most want to be, and end up being" (*The Message*).

Someone can be dirt poor financially and still be the richest person on earth.

Through the years, I've known people who have been blessed with financial wealth. My observation is that the happiest ones are those who have learned to give most of it away. What you give to God and His work now is like making a deposit in heaven. Every dollar you give so that a missionary can go out and share the Gospel has a priceless return when someone comes to know Christ as a result. Can you say that your most valuable assets are in heaven right now? Have you invested your time, energy and resources there already? Knowing Jesus as the "pearl of great price" is worth liquidating everything else in your life. When you do that, your treasure is in heaven where no stock market plunge or double-dip recession can touch it.

Death is Coming

What you give to God and His work now is like making a deposit in heaven.

Jesus doesn't say exactly how the farmer became so successful. We can assume that he earned his wealth by the sweat of his brow and genuine hard work. There isn't anything in the story to make us believe he cheated, lied or stole from someone else to earn his riches. As far as we know, God alone was aware of the depth of his greed. To others, he likely appeared to have it all together. Until one night.

Picture the farmer staying up late one night planning for his future (as he did most nights). Suddenly, there's a knock at the door.

"Who is it?" he calls out.

The answer comes quickly, "It's Death. I've come for you tonight." Death begins an ominous countdown,

"Ten, nine, eight ..."

"Go away, I'm not ready for you! Nobody warned me you were coming!"

Death is now standing in the room before him. "Oh, yes," he says with a wry smile. "I warned you. Do you remember your brother who died of cancer? What about the teenager who drowned in the lake last summer? That was a warning that one day I was coming for you, too." He begins slowly counting down again, "Seven, six, five ..."

Success in God's eyes is when you have a good relationship with Him...

The frightened farmer jumps up from the table full of ledgers and bank statements and cries, "Wait! I'll give you half of my money...just go away!"

Death ignores his plea. "...four, three, two ..."

"Okay!" he screams. "I'll give you ALL my money!"

"...one, zero..."

The next morning, his wife discovers her husband slumped across his expansion blueprints. At his funeral, his friends and co-workers eulogize him as a wonderful man, a community leader and a fine businessman. They bury him in an expensive casket with his name engraved on a polished tombstone. That night, God sends an angel into the cemetery to inscribe four letters on the tombstone: F-O-O-L.

Before he was killed by the Auca Indians in

Ecuador, missionary Jim Elliot wrote in his journal: "He is no fool to give up that which he cannot keep in order to gain that which he can *never* lose!" If you have a growing personal relationship with Jesus Christ, you are rich toward God, and that is something you can never lose! Success in God's eyes is when you have a good relationship with Him, which produces a good relationship with other people. God describes earthly success in Jeremiah 9:23: "The Lord says: 'Let not the wise man boast of his wisdom or the strong man boast of his strength or the rich man boast of his riches, but let him who boasts boast about this: that he understands and knows me, that I am the Lord, who exercises kindness, justice and righteousness on earth, for in these I delight.'"

"...let him who boasts boast about this: that he understands and knows me..."

Although this parable is about the inevitability of death, Jesus had a lot more to say about life. He said the very reason why He came was to give us a more abundant life. He is not out to strip our lives of every material possession like monks in a monastery! He told this parable simply to emphasize that a person's life is not determined by an abundance of possessions. When Jesus spoke of the kind of life He offers, He didn't use the word *bios,* where we get our word *biology*. He offers more than physical existence, because we're all going to die one day. He used the word *zoa* for life, which describes a "quality of living." When we trust Christ, we gain a life with no end that begins here for the rest of our days on earth and extends through eternity.

QUESTIONS TO THINK ABOUT

How does our society define success? How does God?

Using God's definition of success, who is the most successful person you know?

Is there anything inherently wrong with being successful? Explain.

What was the rich fool's chief mistake?

How can materialism negatively affect our enjoyment in life?

Are you afraid to die? Explain your answer.

How are you experiencing the abundant life Jesus promises?

CHAPTER 4
Excuses, Excuses

The Parable of the Dinner Party the Guests Would Not Attend
Luke 14:16-24

They were late again. No one in the classroom was surprised, not even the professor who had seen this freshmen foursome slide into his class late all semester. Each week, the four guys burst through the door, casually mumbled another plausible excuse why they were late and took their seats long after class had started. On the day of the final exam, they arrived just about the time everyone else was finishing. Giggling, they told the professor a dramatic tale about how they'd had a flat tire that morning. Since class was nearly over, they asked if they could take a make-up test later. The professor said, "I'll do better than that. Just have a seat in the four corners of the classroom and I'll prepare a special final exam just for you. I'll make it so easy that you only have to answer one question." The guys looked at each other in surprise and smiled. The professor continued as he passed out a piece of paper to each young man, "If all four of you answer this question correctly, you will all receive an A for the semester. However, if any one of you misses it, you'll all fail." The four guys were still grinning when he handed them their paper, but their smiles disappeared when they turned over the sheets. The single question on the final exam stared them in the face: "Which tire was flat?"

There is a difference between a reason and an excuse.

There is a difference between a reason and an excuse. There are times when we may have a legitimate reason for what we do or don't do. An excuse, however, is like a grape. It has the skin of a reason, but it's stuffed with a lie. In this parable, Jesus talked about the ridiculous excuses we make for not doing what God asks us to do.

He had just told a brief parable about how *not* to behave at a dinner party, in preparation for attending the great wedding feast that God will host in heaven one day. Someone in the crowd remarked aloud how fortunate someone would be to eat with God. (At least you'd think so, anyway.) Who wouldn't want to go to a party thrown by the God of the Universe Himself, right? But Jesus told this next parable to upend that assumption. Turns out, God actually hears more excuses than RSVPs when He issues His invitation.

> For there was once a man who threw a great dinner party and invited many. When it was time for dinner, he sent out his servant to the invited guests, saying, "Come on in; the food's on the table."
>
> Then they all began to beg off, one after another making excuses. The first said, "I bought a piece of property and need to look it over. Send my regrets."
>
> Another said, "I just bought five teams of oxen, and I really need to check them out. Send my regrets."
>
> And yet another said, "I just got married and need to get home to my wife."
>
> The servant went back and told the master what had happened. He was outraged and told the servant, "Quickly, get out into the city streets and alleys. Collect all who look like they need a square meal, all the misfits and homeless and wretched you can lay your hands on, and bring them here."
>
> The servant reported back, "Master, I did what you commanded—and there's still room."
>
> The master said, "Then go to the country roads. Whoever you find, drag them in. I want my house full! Let me tell you, not one of those originally invited is going to get so much as a bite at my dinner party." (***The Message,*** Luke 14:16-24)

God actually hears more excuses than RSVPs when He issues His invitation.

The Meaning of a Parable

Keep in mind how studying a parable of Jesus is similar to peeling an onion. Each story usually has several layers of application. The outer layer is the plot of the story; another layer is what it meant to listeners in Jesus' day; the heart of the parable is the personal application that applies to everyone.

In this case, the basic story is about a rich man who invited people to a wedding feast. However, look at the next layer of historical significance. The lesson spoken to Jesus' original audience was not lost on the Jewish leaders who were listening that day. They knew Jesus was talking about His chosen people, the Jews, who refused His invitation to come to Him. What infuriated them most was the point in the story where the dinner host then invited "the nobodies" to take their place at the party. That meant the God of Israel would invite non-Jews, the Gentiles, to come into His family, which is exactly what Jesus did. Those were fighting words to the Jews who thought they were the only ones worthy of God's attention! The third layer in this parable is the personal application: God is hosting a feast of celebration one day in heaven, and you are invited! How will you respond?

> **How will you respond?**

The *Guinness Book of World Records* claims the biggest and most expensive wedding in modern history took place in Dubai several years ago when an Arab prince married his bride in a 10-day wedding celebration that cost $44 million. A Saudi wedding may be extravagant, but nobody enjoys a wedding celebration more than the Jewish culture! According to custom in Jesus' time, the wedding invitation itself marked the start of the celebration. The host sent the invitation to his guests far in advance, but he did not set the date for the dinner. Each guest would simply agree to come and wait for the host's servant to go out on the appointed day to announce that the banquet was finally ready.

> **It's no accident that Jesus chose a wedding feast to represent what it's like to be with God.**

It's no accident that Jesus chose a wedding feast—the most joyous event in Jewish culture—to represent what it's like to be with God. However, many people mistakenly think the Christian life is anything but a party. They picture it as a boring, sad existence where smiles are frowned upon. (From over 40 years of standing behind a pulpit and looking into the faces of those who claim to be Christians, I have an idea how lost people came up with this notion!) Believers who have lost the joy of their salvation look more like they're waiting for a funeral to start, instead of enjoying a feast with all-you-can-eat Bread of Life and free refills of Living Water!

Vance Havner once said, "I could never understand why some Christians could go to a ball game on Saturday and yell like a bunch of wild Indians, and then go to church the next day and sit like a bunch of wooden Indians! Too many church services start at eleven o'clock sharp and end at twelve o'clock dull." A joyless, gloomy Christian is a contradiction of terms! Instead of *enduring* religion, start *enjoying* a relationship with Him (and then inform your face so it will reflect this change!). The feast God invites us to share with Him includes saucers of salvation, the fruit of forgiveness, kegs of kindness, jugs of joy, platters of peace, layers of love and dishes of devotion. It is filling, but—best of all—it's free!

> **Instead of *enduring* religion, start *enjoying* a relationship with Jesus.**

Come On In!

I have discovered that most other world religions consider their god to be a powerful deity who is not to be disturbed. Therefore, they perform religious acts and rituals so they won't arouse his anger. They are happy if their god never notices them. It's as if they hear their god saying, "Run from me." And they do!

The God of the Bible communicates just the opposite.

In fact, one of God's favorite words is, "Come." Throughout the Bible, He invites people to Himself. When God prepared to destroy wicked humanity with a flood, He directed Noah to build an ark (a picture of His protective presence). When the waters of judgment came, God called to Noah in Genesis 7:2, "COME into the ark...'" Noah and his family sought refuge in the very arms of God inside the ark. In Isaiah 1:18, God says to rebellious men and women, "COME now, let us reason together...though your sins be as scarlet, they shall be as white as snow..." Jesus says, "COME to me all you who are weary and burdened and I will give you rest," Matthew 11:28. On the last page of the Bible, God gives one final invitation: "The Spirit and the Bride say, 'COME!' And let him who hears say, 'COME!' Whoever is thirsty, let him COME..." Revelation 22:17. From Genesis to Revelation, God extends His invitation to come to Him, but many who hear Him calling out to them make up reasons to refuse Him.

> **Jesus says, "COME to me all you who are weary and burdened and I will give you rest."**

Making Excuses

Remember, in Jesus' parable the invitation to the dinner party had already been extended and accepted weeks earlier. However, when it was time to actually go, the guests began to make lame excuses at the last minute. Even today in the Middle East it is an egregious insult to decline an invitation from a great man. However, our culture has refined the art of making excuses. The Metropolitan Insurance Company has published a list of actual automobile accident reports where people try to explain the reason why they had an accident. No wonder they say the truth is stranger than fiction:

(1) "An invisible car came out of nowhere, struck my car, and vanished."

(2) "The pedestrian had no idea which direction to go, so I ran over him."

(3) "I had been driving for 40 years when I fell asleep at the wheel and had the accident."

(4) "The indirect cause was a little guy in a small car with a big mouth."

(5) "The other driver was all over the road. I had to swerve a number of times before I hit him."

(6) "I pulled away from the side of the road, glanced at my mother-in-law, and headed over the embankment."

Today, you don't even have to make up your own excuses. The Internet will do it for you. Did you know there are websites suggesting hundreds of excuses you can give for any situation? For instance, there are excuses to use if you are caught sleeping at work. If your boss awakens you, just say, "They told me at the blood bank that this might happen." Or, they suggested opening your eyes and simply saying, "Amen."

The three excuses Jesus shared in His parable are the same excuses people still give God today. He'd already heard these kinds of excuses a million times over the course of human history; that's why He told this story. On the surface, the excuses each character in the story gave appeared to be legitimate. However, at the end of the day, they simply didn't want to do what He asked. Where do you see yourself in these examples?

> Excuse #1: I've got to take care of my stuff!

Excuse #1: I've got to take care of my stuff!

The first man said he just bought some land and he had to examine it. I don't buy that excuse. How many people would purchase real estate sight unseen? If you would, I have some prime oceanfront property in the Texas Panhandle that I want to sell you! This man represents people who are irrationally preoccupied with their possessions. Have you ever noticed that the more stuff you have, the more stuff you need to take care of the things you have? Some people are so enthralled with their gadgets that they are controlled by them. Have you ever seen someone bump into something or someone while they're walking and trying to text, surf the Web or talk on their smartphone—all at the same time? We spend most of our lives buying more new stuff to take the place of our old stuff. Then we have to spend the rest of our time using, protecting and upgrading all our stuff. Jesus said, "A man's life does not consist of the abundance of his possessions" (Luke 12:15). Has an abundance of technology overtaken the free time in your life? The time you used to spend reading your Bible or talking with God in prayer?

> Has an abundance of technology overtaken the free time in your life?

Excuse #2: My job keeps me too busy!

The second party guest indicated he just purchased five teams of oxen, so he was going out to test-drive them. After all, it was essential to his work that these oxen do a good job, right? The first problem with this excuse is that it was dinnertime—almost dark. Was he planning to practice glow-in-the-dark plowing? I don't think so. It was just another lame excuse. No wonder the host became angry and frustrated.

Many people claim they don't have time for God because they stay so busy with their jobs. They are so consumed by their workload that they can't squeeze God into their busy schedule. I've known folks who used to serve God, but they became so successful in their jobs that they no longer had time to serve the Lord in their church.

Dr. R.G. Lee tells the story about a young man who was a faithful servant in their church. Bob was also a business genius and started a single retail store that was so successful he soon expanded and became a millionaire. However, he was so busy with his growing business that he never had time for God anymore. Dr. Lee noticed Bob and his family stopped working in the church and only made it to worship once a month, if that. One day, Dr. Lee decided to visit Bob at his office. He walked right past the receptionist into Bob's office. Bob was surprised to see his pastor, but he welcomed him to sit down. Dr. Lee got right to the point and said, "Bob, I've come by to pray for your business." Before Bob could reply, Dr. Lee led him to his knees and began to pray aloud, "Lord, I pray that You'll make Bob's business fail..."

Excuse #2: My job keeps me too busy!

At that, Bob's head jerked up, but Dr. Lee kept right on praying! "I pray that You'll take away all those other stores and just give him his original store because You remember, Lord, how much He loved You and served You before he got too busy for You. In Jesus' name, Amen." When Dr. Lee finished, Bob said, "Dr. Lee, I didn't really like that prayer." Dr. Lee, in his typical bold manner, just said, "That's okay, Bob. I wasn't talking to you, anyway. See you Sunday." That prayer got Bob's attention, and he started making God's work a higher priority than his retail business. He and his family began serving God again, and instead of losing his business, it grew. Are you using your job as an excuse for not giving God 100% of your life? Everyone always thinks they'll "just take a time-out" from serving and return when things calm down. However, very few make it back to serving God once they make that initial decision. Do you think that God blesses your business so that you can serve Him less?

Do you think that God blesses your business so that you can serve Him less?

Excuse #3: My family takes up my time!

I picture a deer-in-the-headlights look on this newlywed's face. He wanted the host to think he'd like to come but his wife wouldn't let him! However, this is just another empty excuse because it was unheard of to invite a man to a wedding feast and not invite his wife. They were both invited, but he did not want to go—so he used his new marriage as a convenient excuse.

Spending time with your family is a noble pursuit. It is a much better investment of your time than other distractions at work. However, even family can get in the way of serving God. Jesus said you cannot follow Him unless you love Him more than your mother or father, brothers or sisters or your spouse and children. Many people choose not to relate to God on a regular basis because they use their Sundays for family outings. The very best family outing is to take your family to worship with you. You can't use your family as an excuse for not coming to God. Actually, there is no legitimate *reason* for not accepting His invitation. Romans 1:20 says, "For since the creation of the world, God's invisible qualities—his eternal power and divine nature—have been clearly seen, being understood from what has been made, so that men are without excuse."

Excuse #3: My family takes up my time!

Inviting Others

Near the end of the story, the attention moves to the interaction between the servant and the master. When the master learned the guests refused to come, he was insulted and angry! But he didn't cancel the party; he just expanded his invitation to include everyone in the region—even the homeless misfits and the poor, crippled, blind and lame. When Jesus got to this part in the story, the self-righteous Pharisees were incredulous. They always thought that people with disadvantages and disabilities meant God was *punishing* them for their sins. In this story, God wants to give them a place of honor at His table instead!

At this point in the parable, our role changes, too. We're no longer the people giving the excuses; we are the servants sent out to gather people for the great feast. We've moved from dinner guest to party planner. After the first rounds of invitations went out on the highways and the by-ways, the servant returned and said, "There is still room." The host sent them out again and told the servants, "Don't just invite them—bring them if you can!" In other words, make an effort to connect with lost people because you cannot reach them at arm's length. Take time to get to know people and start building relationships. This is what people often call "friendship evangelism." If you want to invite someone to church with you, offer to pick him or her up. According to research, the number one reason why people attend a church for the first time is because of a friend.

> **...We are the servants sent out to gather people for the great feast.**

Here is what I think the heavenly invitation from God, engraved with the blood of Christ, says. Consider your own response, and then commit to share the invitation with others.

You are cordially invited to the
banquet of My salvation.

Serving will begin at My House
and will continue for eternity.

Dress: Come just as you are.
Hosted by: God Almighty

Every Christian is like a heavenly postman, delivering the invitation God has issued to every zip code in the world.

QUESTIONS TO THINK ABOUT

What is the best wedding you ever attended and why?

Why did the guests in this story make excuses?

When was a time you excused yourself from serving God in a certain capacity?

How do you allow God to prioritize your time between your relationship with Him and family, church and work?

What would you need to subtract and/or add to your schedule in order to be more balanced?

How do others typically respond when you share God's invitation to experience grace? What encourages you about their response? What discourages you?

How can you creatively issue God's invitation in your community?

CHAPTER 5
How to Cultivate a Teachable Heart

The Parable of the Sower
Luke 8:5-15

Unless you grew up on a farm, you might not know what the word *cultivate* means. You may envision plowing behind a team of oxen. Or maybe you picture people hunched over rows of plowed earth dropping seeds into the ground or working a harvest. Actually, it doesn't mean to plow, or plant or reap. To *cultivate* means to break up the soil around growing plants in order to destroy weeds and improve the soil's moisture. That farming term has come to mean the careful development of any preference, such as, "I have cultivated a taste for classical music." It's something that takes work on our part.

Unlike today, everyone in Jesus' audience at that time knew something about farming because it was an agricultural society. In fact, the Bible is full of agricultural themes. Jesus chose a parable about farming to show us how to be a good listener of the Word and "cultivate" a teachable heart. A verse in the Old Testament gives us a picture of what that means in a spiritual sense. In Hosea 10:12, God says, "Reap the fruit of unfailing love, and break up your unplowed ground; for it is time to seek the Lord, until He comes and showers righteousness on you." Here is the story Jesus told to further illustrate this idea:

Are you listening to this? Really listening?

A farmer went out to sow his seed. Some of it fell on the road; it was tramped down and the birds ate it. Other seed fell in the gravel; it sprouted, but withered because it didn't have good roots. Other seed fell in the weeds; the weeds grew with it and strangled it. Other seed fell in rich earth and produced a bumper crop.

[Jesus said], Are you listening to this? Really listening?

His disciples asked, "Why did you tell this story?"

You've been given insight into God's kingdom—you know how it works. There are others who need stories. But even with stories some of them aren't going to get it: Their eyes are open but don't see a thing, their ears are open but don't hear a thing. This story is about some of those people.

The seed is the Word of God. The seeds on the road are those who hear the Word, but no sooner do they hear it than the Devil snatches it from them so they won't believe and be saved.

The seeds in the gravel are those who hear with enthusiasm, but the enthusiasm doesn't go very deep. It's only another fad, and the moment there's trouble it's gone.

And the seed that fell in the weeds—well, these are the ones who hear, but then the seed is crowded out and nothing comes of it as they go about their lives worrying about tomorrow, making money, and having fun.

But the seed in the good earth—these are the good-hearts who seize the Word and hold on no matter what, sticking with it until there's a harvest. (***The Message,*** Luke 8:5-15)

It's all about the Word of God and the attitude with which we approach what God says to us.

Jesus followed His story with an immediate explanation of what it meant, something He didn't always do when He told a parable. We know from His explanation that the point of the parable is *not* seeds and dirt. It's all about the Word of God and the attitude with which we approach what God says to us.

Some scholars debate whether the four soil conditions described in this story portray four different people. They usually suggest the first soil is an unbeliever and the final soil is a believer who responds to God's Word. However, that doesn't account for the other two categories in the middle of the story. Some erroneously say these represent Christians who lost their salvation. (I don't believe the Bible teaches that a Christian can lose his or her salvation.) Others insist they are backslidden Christians.

I think that entire debate misses the point. I suggest these are not four different people; they are four different attitudes of the human heart. It's possible for each of us to reflect all four attitudes at different times in our lives. The great Bible expositor, Ray Stedman, wrote: "I used to read this story as though these various soils were four different kinds of people, who remained the same all through their lifetimes—some were permanently hard-hearted, like the first example given; some were impulsive, some were full of concerns. But I have come to see that what our Lord is describing here is not four types of persons, so much, but conditions of our heart at any given moment. Whenever the Word is being taught, people are in one condition or another, just as they are described to us here. We have all been callous, at times. We have all been impulsive in our reaction—emotional and shallow. We have all been overly concerned about other matters. And we have all had times of being open and responsive to the Word."

We have all been impulsive in our reaction—emotional and shallow.

Instead of trying to figure out who is saved or lost in the story, instead examine your own heart and see which of these four attitudes characterize your life *right now.*

A Hard Heart

> The seeds on the road are those who hear the Word, but no sooner do they hear it than the Devil snatches it from them so they won't believe and be saved.

Most Jewish people learned Scripture from a young age. However, others "needed stories" about God's truth, Jesus explained, because they did not have access to the Scriptures. And yet, this parable seemed to go over everyone's heads—even the disciples, who had to ask Him to explain it. Jesus said, "You've been given insight into God's kingdom—you know how it works. There are others who need stories. But even with stories some of them aren't going to get it: Their eyes are open but don't see a thing. Their ears are open but don't hear a thing" (8:10).

> **"Their ears are open but don't hear a thing."**

It's no surprise that the first soil in Jesus' story is about people who just don't get it, when it comes to hearing and understanding God's Word. They don't consider themselves to be hard-hearted people. In fact, they can be some of the nicest people in your family, neighborhood or workplace. They simply aren't interested in church, religion and especially not the Word of God. Their heart is like a pathway that has been trampled down until the dirt surrounding it is hard-packed. Whatever they may hear about God may enter their ears, but it certainly never enters their hearts.

It's not entirely their fault, however. Jesus explains there is a something going on in the background, invisible to the human eye, which makes it even harder to receive the Word of God. Jesus says Satan tries to "steal" the Word. Those listening to Jesus tell this story knew it was a common sight to see a flock of birds swarming around a farmer as he tossed his seed.

One of the enemy's most effective strategies is distraction.

In the same way, the devil stands poised to try to steal the Word away from people as soon as they hear it. Remember, this soil is not exclusive to describing non-Christians. He can steal away even a believer's attention from the Word of God. Don't ever be surprised if you have trouble concentrating when you are reading the Bible or when you are hearing the Bible being taught. One of the enemy's most effective strategies is distraction. That's why you may sense your mind wandering to what you're going to do later in the afternoon when you are at church. It can explain why you keep thinking of other things when you are trying to pray or concentrate on reading your Bible. Remember, spiritual warfare is real, and it starts long before you accept Christ and continues throughout your life as a Christian, too. In fact, it may even increase!

A Shallow Heart

> The seeds in the gravel are those who hear with enthusiasm, but the enthusiasm doesn't go very deep. It's only another fad, and the moment there's trouble it's gone.

Jesus said the second kind of attitude starts by receiving the Word of God with joy. These people react with an emotional acceptance of the Word. I've seen many people in church smile, shout "amen" and even shed a few tears of joy as they experience a Sunday morning worship service. By Tuesday morning, these same folks are downcast and defeated. The emotion is gone, and so is their commitment. They could be called "Alka-Seltzer" hearers of the Word—they fizzle furiously for a short while and then they fade away. Jesus issues this warning to us about the danger of basing our Christian faith on our emotions. No doubt, sometimes a message or a worship song can move us inside and create a wonderful feeling of satisfaction and fulfillment. We are aware God loves us, everything is great and our faith is strong. For some people, the

We are aware God loves us, everything is great and our faith is strong.

reason they come to church is to get a "spiritual fix" to last them through the week so they can come back next week and get a refill.

As a pastor, it is not my desire to touch one's emotions each week; I'm trying to build healthy Christians who are fully devoted, mature followers of Christ. I believe God has called me to be a pastor so I can consistently feed others the meat of the Word of God Sunday after Sunday. I don't often preach "emotionally stirring" messages in a sweat-soaked suit. In fact, I rarely wear a suit! We all love ice cream, but if we ate it every meal, it would soon get old. Christmas is wonderful, but if it were Christmas every day, it would soon be disappointing. Be careful that you don't come to church just looking for a thrill—that's what Six Flags is for.

When life turns up the heat, you need more than just an emotional faith.

Don't get me wrong. I believe we should love God with our entire being, our mind, our wills and our emotions. But your emotions are the shallowest part of your soul.

You may be wondering, "But I want to feel good about God! What's wrong with an emotional faith?" That kind of attitude doesn't stand up under the heat. Trouble and testing come into our lives like the keen rays of the sun; an emotionally driven faith won't pass the test. In this parable, the plant had no root, so it withered and died under the difficulty. When life turns up the heat, you need more than just an emotional faith. You need deep roots that will nourish your soul with the Living Water.

Have you ever described someone as being "grounded"? That person is usually very secure emotionally and not easily angered or upset by circumstances. Are you "rooted and grounded" in the Word of God? The massive redwood trees on the Pacific coast are majestic to see. They soar to amazing heights, but they have surprisingly short roots. The reason why is because the roots of each tree are intertwined with the roots of the other trees around it. That's why you never see a redwood standing alone; it cannot support itself. What a beautiful picture of the Church—believers holding each other together to stand strong in the midst of life's difficulties.

Are you "rooted and grounded" in the Word of God?

A Crowded Heart

> And the seed that fell in the weeds—well, these are the ones who hear, but then the seed is crowded out and nothing comes of it as they go about their lives worrying about tomorrow, making money, and having fun.

It's my opinion this third category characterizes the attitude of more people than the first two combined.

I believe this kind of person has a genuine desire to be a deeply rooted, maturing Christian. However, somewhere along the way something interrupts their growth process and thwarts their potential. They allow their lives to become so crowded with other interests that the impact of the Word of God gets choked out.

If you know anything about gardening, you know there is a limited amount of moisture and nutrients in soil. Weeds and thorns compete for these nutrients with the good plants you are trying to grow, which is why all wise gardeners provide additional food and water for their plants. Likewise, some things in our lives compete for our affection for the Word of God. Like weeds, these things are very common to all humans—worries, wealth and wants. And like weeds, if you aren't careful, these things will choke out the effectiveness of God's Word in your heart.

> **Worry is like a weed that spreads until it has overrun the field.**

Strangled by Worries

Our English Word *worry* comes from the German Word *wurgen*, which means "to choke." Worry is the devil's mental and emotional chokehold on a believer. I'm convinced the most prevalent sin among Christians is worry. No matter how much Scripture you know, worry will always displace it and diffuse its power to calm your fears. In Jesus' story, worry is like a weed that spreads until it has overrun the field.

There are two categories of troubles, (1) Those you can't do anything about it; and (2) Those you can do something about. If you can't do anything about your trouble, then why worry? If you *can* do something, don't worry—do something! I once read a folk rhyme about worry:

For every evil under the sun;
Either there is a cure;
or there is none.
If there be one,
seek 'till you find it.
If there be none,
never mind it!

If you can't do anything about your trouble, then why worry?

Strangled by Wealth

A better translation of this is found in Matthew 13:22 where Jesus warns about the "deceitfulness of wealth." There is nothing inherently evil in money, but wealth can fool you into having a false sense of security and self-worth. Thinking you can buy your way into and out of any situation has been the downfall of many a wealthy person.

On August 16, 1977, Elvis Presley died from complications of drug usage. At Graceland (his personal home that draws over a quarter of a million people every year), his motorcycles and Cadillacs are all on display, including his private jets he named Hound Dog II and the Lisa Marie. Elvis loved to fly around the country late at night just to satisfy a craving for things like a special kind of peanut butter sold only in Denver.

Elvis' younger stepbrother, Rick Stanley, spoke many times at a church I pastored in Alabama. Rick said he thought his brother really loved Jesus at one time, noting that his favorite style of music was always gospel music. According to Rick, Elvis' biggest mistake was allowing all the fame and money to choke out the Word of God in his life. You don't have to be as rich and famous as Elvis for that to happen to you. If you love gold more than God, the Word will get choked out. Over time, Jesus becomes just one of several good interests in your life.

> **If you love gold more than God, the Word will get choked out.**

Strangled by Wants

Jesus said some people are distracted by "having fun," as *The Message* paraphrase terms it—but don't confuse having fun with sin! In fact, Christians ought to be the ones enjoying this life to the full, just as Jesus desired (John 10:10). Yet when you make your pursuit of "good times" your entire focus, you lose sight of your priorities. Other translations use the word "pleasures"—loving the things the world has to offer. It all comes down to what you desire most…your "wants." Do you desire the Word of God throughout your day, or are you preoccupied with surfing online shopping sites to add more items to your wish list? Did you expect the last purchase you made or trip you took to satisfy that deep longing in your heart that only God can fulfill? If you did, you were surely disappointed after a while.

The saddest part of Jesus' story is that the one with this attitude of worry, wealth and wants *really* wanted to receive the Word and be fruitful. He isn't hard hearted, or shallow minded; he just allowed other things to crowd out the Word of God like weeds in an unattended field. Is this person going to heaven? Probably. What's the downside then? Jesus says of that person's potential "nothing comes of it." In another translation, v14 says: "…they do not mature." A busy, distracted, over-extended Christian is relegated to a sad life on earth of lost potential and perpetual spiritual immaturity.

Would you like to have an open, teachable heart?

A Teachable Heart

> But the seed in the good earth—these are the good-hearts who seize the Word and hold on no matter what, sticking with it until there's a harvest.

Would you like to have an open, teachable heart? It doesn't come automatically; it must be *cultivated* by breaking up the hardened earth around your heart and removing the weeds. A teachable heart receives the Word of God into soft, fertile soil and produces a bumper crop of unfailing love. There are four practical ways to cultivate this kind of attitude:

Cultivate a Hunger for the Word!

> **If you hunger for the Word, you will show up at the appointed time for the meal.**

The Psalmist observed, "How sweet are your words to my taste, sweeter than honey to my mouth" Psalm 119:105. Do you have a voracious appetite and desire to read and hear God's Word? Sadly, many of us find ourselves more interested in our next physical meal than we are in hearing from God.

The French speak an interesting phrase whenever you sit down to eat a meal. They say, *Bon appétit,* which means "good appetite." Why don't they say, *Good food* at the start of the meal? They understand your enjoyment of a meal is directly related to the intensity of your appetite, not necessarily the quality of the food. If you haven't eaten in two days, a bowl of soup tastes heavenly. On the other hand, you can sit down to the finest meal prepared by the most talented chef, but if you've just eaten three Big Macs, you won't enjoy more than a couple of bites. Why? You are already full.

If you don't hunger for the Word of God, it is likely because you are already full from indulging in something else. It says much more about your own lack of spiritual appetite than about the quality of the food. For example, a person who truly hungers for the Word never debates on Saturday night, "Am I going to church tomorrow?" That question is as superfluous as asking, "Am I going to eat today?" If you hunger for the Word, you will show up at the appointed time for the meal.

"He who has ears to hear, let him hear!"

Practice Intentional Listening

For many years, the RCA logo was a dog sitting in front of a gramophone with one ear cocked, listening for his master's voice. That iconic picture also describes those whose attention is always turned heavenward to hear what God has to say to them.

During a lifetime of preaching, I've looked into the faces of some people who don't seem to be really listening for God. It's as if they put mental signs around their necks that read, "DO NOT DISTURB." That's why Jesus prefaced this story with the challenge: "He who has ears to hear, let him hear!" Luke 8:8 (NIV). Huh? Didn't everybody there have ears? But not everyone who *can* hear really *listens* to God. In *The Message* paraphrase it reads: "Are you listening to this? REALLY listening?"

Chuck Swindoll tells the story about a Native American walking in downtown New York City alongside a friend who lived there. Right in the center of Manhattan, with taxis blaring their horns and the subway roaring, the visitor stopped suddenly and said, "Wait! I hear a cricket!" His New Yorker friend couldn't believe it, but sure enough his friend traced the cricket to a large cement planter several yards from where they were standing. He held up the little creature, obviously delighted with his find! "How did you do that?" his friend wanted to know. He answered that it "depends on what you're listening for." Then he reached into his pocket, pulled out some coins and, raising his hand waist high, dropped them on the sidewalk. Every head on the street turned and looked in the direction of the coins (*Living on the Ragged Edge*, p.37). When you are reading the Bible, or hearing it taught, do you aggressively tune out the distractions and tune in to what God is saying? It depends on what you're listening for!

> A good listener not only *hears* the Word but also *retains* it.

Retaining What You Read

Jesus gets very practical at this point in the story when He said a good listener not only *hears* the Word but also *retains* it. I like the verb phrases *The Message* paraphrase uses: *seize it, hold onto it, stick with it.* Remember all the math formulas and dates in history you memorized when you were in school? Of course you don't! If you were like most students, you crammed in some information right before an exam so you could regurgitate it onto a piece of paper in class. Memorizing Scripture takes a different approach. The Psalmist said, "I have hidden your Word in my heart that I might not sin against you," Psalm 119:11. If you "hide it in your heart," it will be with you for a lifetime.

"I have hidden your Word in my heart that I might not sin against you."

Another way to retain the Word is to take notes whenever you hear it taught. For years, I have made a practice of taking notes whenever I hear a message on the Bible. I have notebooks full of sermon notes I've taken from other people. I can take out those well-worn pages and be blessed again and again by the Word. Studies have shown that 24 hours after you hear something, you will only remember 10% of it unless you take notes. Writing it down allows you to recall over 40% of what you heard.

Einstein was correct when he said, "A short pencil is better than a long memory." If a doctor came into your hospital room after surgery and told you three things you needed to do to get well, you'd be scrambling to write it down. Try to write down everything God reveals to you through His Word, times of prayer and messages you hear others teach.

Help Others Hear the Word

We are now the farmer, spreading seeds of God's Word to others.

Jesus said having a teachable heart is like working fertile soil that produces a crop that reproduces itself in a harvest. As any farmer knows, good soil not only produces crops; it produces more seed that can be replanted. When I plant okra seeds in our garden every summer, I always have more than enough. So, I keep the extra pods dry to replant the seeds the following year. That's how it works with okra—but what about the "harvest" someone is able to produce, spiritually speaking?

At this point in the story, our perspective changes again (something Jesus often did in His parables). We are no longer represented in the soils—we are now the farmer, spreading seeds of God's Word to others. There is a beautiful picture from Psalm 126:6 about a sower and seeds. It says, "He who goes out weeping, carrying seed to sow will return with songs of joy, carrying sheaves with him." When you have a teachable heart, your heart is so broken for those who don't know Jesus that you literally weep as you plant seeds of the Word in their lives through your testimony, a kind act in Jesus' name or sharing the Gospel.

Notice that the farmer in Jesus' story was so generous with his seed that he didn't plant it in only the fertile ground. He tossed it everywhere, knowing that only a quarter of the seed would be successful. Don't be stingy with the Word of God—spread it around and leave the results to God. Sometimes when I'm traveling on a plane I'll slip a thin booklet about the Gospel between the pages of a magazine for others to find. I try to pick a popular article like, "How to Make a Million Dollars before Friday." I'm just planting seeds, and I know most will toss it when the flight attendant comes down the aisle holding a trash bag. I won't be a bit surprised, however, to get to heaven and find somebody who says, "I was saved by reading a booklet about the Gospel that I found on an airline flight!"

The seed of the Word is so powerful all you have to do is plant it—God will do the rest.

The seed of the Word is so powerful all you have to do is plant it—God will do the rest. Dr. Gaylord

Kambarami, who served as the General Secretary for the International Bible Society in Zimbabwe, told a story about passing out New Testaments in a crowd one day. A very skeptical man told him if he took a Bible, he would just tear out the pages and roll them up to make cigarettes. Dr. Kambarami told him to take a Bible anyway, but he made him promise to read each page before he smoked it.

Years later, he met the same man at a Christian convention. The one-time Scripture-smoking man was now an evangelist! He explained to Dr. Kambarami, "I smoked my way through Matthew, Mark and Luke, but when I got to John 3:16, I couldn't smoke anymore. When I read that, I got on my knees, and that's when Jesus changed my life!" No matter what kind of soil is around your heart, God can break up the compacted dirt and breathe life into it again as He did when He created Adam from the dust. From that point on, you are in the farming business—spreading seeds to share with others.

You are in the farming business—spreading seeds to share with others.

QUESTIONS TO THINK ABOUT

How would you describe the 4 soils in this parable in your own words?

How can a Christian reflect all 4 soils (attitudes) at various times?

Which soil do you relate to most often? Why?

What distracts you most from taking time to read your Bible consistently?

Do you have a teachable heart? Explain.

What would improve your ability to listen to and retain more of what you learn about the Bible?

Where are you currently planting seeds of God's Word in others?

CHAPTER 6

That's Not FAIR! No, That's Grace.

The Parable of the Great Reversal
Matthew 20:1-16

One of the thousands of urban myths spread by email involves Microsoft founder, Bill Gates, as a commencement speaker at a high school graduation where he supposedly shared a speech entitled: "Life Rules They Don't Teach You in High School." Bill Gates has done a lot of things in his lifetime, but he never made that speech! California educator, Dr. Charles Sykes, actually created this clever set of rules, and they apply to those of us far beyond high school, too!

Life Rules They Don't Teach You in High School

Rule 7: Television is not real life. In real life, people actually have to leave the coffee shop and go to jobs.

Rule 6: Life is not divided into semesters. You don't get summers off, and very few employers are interested in helping you find yourself. Do that on your own time.

Rule 5: If you mess up, it's not your parents' fault. So, don't whine about your mistakes. Learn from them.

Rule 4: Flipping burgers is not beneath your dignity. Your grandparents had a different word for burger-flipping; they called it opportunity.

Rule 3: If you think your teacher is tough, wait until you get a boss. He doesn't have tenure.

Rule 2: Be nice to nerds. Chances are you'll end up working for one. (That's probably why the list was attributed to Bill Gates.)

Rule 1: Life is not fair. So get used to it.
(based on *50 Rules Kids Won't Learn in School,* Dr. Charles Sykes, 2007)

When Dr. Sykes was asked how he felt to know that everyone from Ann Landers to Paul Harvey wrongly attributed his list to Bill Gates he quoted his own rule: Life is not fair! He notes the average teenager uses the phrase, "It's not fair!" 8.6 times a day. Those of you with teenagers may be nodding your heads, but Dr. Sykes says the kids got it from their baby boomer parents—the most idealistic generation.

If you ask me, it's not fair that some people can eat gallons of ice cream without gaining a pound. It's not fair that one high-school dropout, coke-snorting Hollywood actor makes more money on one bad movie than all the high school teachers in my city combined. The list goes on and on. "*I've been with this company for years, and that young upstart gets the promotion? It's not fair!*" "*I raised my child to know Jesus, and now he has turned against God. It's not fair!*" "*I've never smoked, and now the doctor tells me I have lung cancer? My uncle smoked a pack a day for 30 years and he's fine. It's just not fair!*"

"But many who are first will be last, and many who are last will be first."

One of the themes of the Bible is the fact that life isn't fair...but God is good. To demonstrate this point, Jesus told it in story form in Matthew 20. Matthew 19 gives us a running start. (The chapter and verse divisions in the Bible were inserted in the 13th century, and sometimes they chose inappropriate places for a break.) Matthew 19:30 and 20:16 provide bookends to Jesus' story. He said, "But many who are first will be last, and many who are last will be first"(19:30). Then He said the same thing but reversed the order in Matthew 20:16: "So the last will be first and the first will be last." He then inserts the following story about a great reversal of fortune between these two "bookend" verses:

> God's kingdom is like an estate manager who went out early in the morning to hire workers for his vineyard. They agreed on a wage of a dollar a day, and went to work. Later, about nine o'clock, the manager saw some other men hanging around the town square unemployed. He told them to go to work in his vineyard and he would pay them a fair wage. They went.
>
> He did the same thing at noon, and again at three o'clock. At five o'clock he went back and found still others standing around. He said, "Why are you standing around all day doing nothing?"
>
> They said, "Because no one hired us."
>
> He told them to go to work in his vineyard.
>
> When the day's work was over, the owner of the vineyard instructed his foreman, "Call the workers in and pay them their wages. Start with the last hired and go on to the first."
>
> Those hired at five o'clock came up and were each given a dollar. When those who were hired first saw that, they assumed they would get far more. But they got the same, each of them one dollar. Taking the dollar, they groused angrily to the manager, "These last workers put in only one easy hour, and you just made them equal to us, who slaved all day under a scorching sun."
>
> He replied to the one speaking for the rest, "Friend, I haven't been unfair. We agreed on the wage of a dollar, didn't we? So take it and go. I decided to give to the one who came last the same as you. Can't I do what I want with my own money? Are you going to get stingy because I am generous?"
>
> Here it is again, the Great Reversal: many of the first ending up last, and the last first. (***The Message,*** Matthew 20:1-16)

The kingdom of heaven uses different math than the world uses. In God's kingdom, He leaves the 99 sheep to go after the one lost one. In God's kingdom, a widow's two pennies are more valuable than all the gold given in the Temple one whole day. The world would call that fuzzy math, but the Bible calls it grace.

In many Bibles, the heading (also inserted as helpful guides long after the Bible was written) reads: The Parable of the Workers. However, it's a misnomer. This parable reveals more about the Generous Boss than the Workers. Eugene Peterson calls it the Parable of the Great Reversal because Jesus works a surprise ending into His story. No matter what you call it, it is a head-scratching story that teaches us about the character of God.

This parable reveals more about the Generous Boss than the Workers.

The Workers

Some of the workers started their day at 6:00am and worked all day. I think those first workers represent Christians who have been serving most of their lives. I'm in that group. I started going to church nine months before I was born because I was blessed with Christian parents. Church has always been an important part of my life. When I was nine years old, I trusted Christ and became a part of God's family.

Studies show that people most often come to Christ at an early age before 18, but on rare occasions some come to Christ late in life. Even more rare are what we call "deathbed conversions." When Jesus was hanging on the cross, a condemned thief asked Him to remember him when He came into His kingdom. That was a powerful profession of faith on his part because Jesus didn't look much like a King at that moment. Jesus assured him that even today, when that man breathed his last breath, he would find himself with Jesus in paradise (Luke 23:39-43). His place in Scripture reminds us that it's never too late to trust Jesus…in this life. If you die without putting your faith in Jesus, then it's definitely too late. Someone observed about this scene that there is one deathbed conversion in the Bible "so nobody should despair," but there is only one, "so nobody should presume."

> **The real pay-off is a personal relationship with Jesus that lasts forever.**

The controversy in this story is that all the workers received the same amount at the end of the workday, no matter what time they started working. Each received a denarius, which was a full day's wage. So what is our "denarius"? If you think, "heaven," wrong answer. Heaven is just one of the benefits of salvation. The real pay-off is a personal relationship with Jesus that lasts forever, starting now. John 17:3 gives us the best definition of eternal life: being with Jesus Himself.

Speaking of His Father, Jesus said: "And this is eternal life, that they may know You, the only true God, and Jesus Christ whom you have sent."

When Jesus said to the thief on the cross: "Today you will be with me in paradise," He put the emphasis on a certain part of that statement, and I think the thief heard it loud and clear. Most people tune into the idea of "paradise." I believe that Jesus focused on "with me" when He spoke those words in a raggedy gasp from the cross. Wherever Jesus is, that's paradise.

Wherever Jesus is, that's paradise.

Jeff Stratton, a pastor in Indiana, received a call one day to visit a ninety-three-year-old man with terminal cancer. Adolph Allen had been a hard-living, hard-drinking, union ironworker for most of his life. Two minutes into their first conversation, Adolph looked at Jeff and asked, "Is it fair for someone to live their whole life one way and then at the end of their life ask God to take them to heaven?" After thinking for a minute, Jeff said, "No, Adolph it's not fair. But luckily for you and me, God is not fair." Jeff shared the plan of salvation with him, and Adolph bowed his gray head and asked Jesus to come into his heart. Four weeks later, Jeff preached Adolph's funeral. He talked about a football game that came down to a final play.

The losing team had been outplayed the whole game, but on the last play the quarterback heaved a Hail Mary pass into the end zone as time expired to win the game. Jeff said, "That's what happened with Adolph. The devil was in the lead for most of his life, but the final score was Jesus 1 and the devil 0!"

The problem with deathbed conversions is that statistics show more people die *out* of bed than *in* a bed.

It's never too late to start serving in God's vineyard. Some people have labored there serving God most of their lives—while others are constantly flooding into it at all times throughout the day and night to start their shift. God is still walking through the vineyard rows of this world inviting everyone, "Come work in my vineyard." If someone's sincere acceptance of Christ sneaks in under the wire amid people who have been working in the vineyard for decades, it's not too late. The Generous Boss will not count them out. That's not fair, but thank God, that's grace.

> **That's not fair, but thank God, that's grace.**

A Lesson about Grace

Let's be honest. Some Christians who have worked in the vineyard all their lives bristle at the equality in this story in the same way that Jesus' original audience of Pharisees did. I imagine they crossed their arms and huffed aloud, causing a small smile to curl on Jesus' lips as He finished His story. Some people try a more theological route to register their dismay. They read this parable and say, "Well, doesn't the Bible say we'll be rewarded for our faithful service to the Lord? And doesn't the Bible say not everyone receives the same rewards?" Yes, there will be "rewards" handed out in the form of crowns when we gather around the throne of the Lamb. However, don't plan on holding onto them; we aren't going to wear those crowns for eternity. In Revelation 4, we learn we're going to cast our crowns before His throne—where they rightfully belong. And, while we're at it, let's clarify the idea that some believers will have a nicer mansion in heaven while others settle for a little cabin on a hilltop. That is not biblical either. The Bible says we'll all be in the Father's house, which has many rooms and room for all.

We'll all be in the Father's house, which has many rooms and room for all.

Writer Phillip Yancey makes this observation about this parable: "The workers' discontent arouse from the scandalous mathematics of grace. They would not accept that their employer had the right to do what he wanted with his money when it meant paying scoundrels twelve times what they deserved. Many

Christians who study this parable identify with the employees who put in a full day's work, rather than the add-ons at the end of the day. We like to think of ourselves as responsible workers, and the employer's strange behavior baffles us as it did the original hearers. We risk missing the story's point: that God dispenses gifts, not wages. If paid on the basis of fairness, we would all end up in hell" (*What's So Amazing About Grace?*, pp.61-62).

> **Eternal life isn't heaven; it is knowing God.**

If it's a wage you want from God, the Bible clearly identifies it in Romans 6:23: "The wages of sin is death..." If you want grace instead, it's a gift that can't be earned—only gladly received. The other half of that verse is: "But the gift of God is eternal life in Christ Jesus our Lord." What is the gift? Again, eternal life isn't heaven; it is knowing God. That's the gift—the full denarius—and everyone in the kingdom receives it all. That's not fair, but thank God, that's grace.

I love the part in the parable where the sweat-covered, 12-hour workers take their complaints to the owner. He just smiles and basically says, "Get over it." Grace (especially when it is dispensed to others) disturbs our sense of justice. Business owners often read this parable and chuckle, "That's no way to run a successful business. It's not how I would go about it anyway." Of course not. God says, "My thoughts are not your thoughts, neither are your ways my ways...as the heavens are higher than the earth, so are my ways higher than your ways and my thoughts higher than your thoughts" (Isaiah 55:8-9).

Michael Sherer had an unusual experience with grace one time in seminary. He stayed up all night studying for a final exam in one of his theology classes. As he entered the classroom, he looked around, smugly noting the nervous looks of the "slackers" he knew did not study much. He had put in the time, however, and was ready to ace the exam. Before the professor passed out the exams, he briefly reviewed some topics that would be on the fill-in-the-blank test. Michael started to panic because those topics weren't in his notes. He immediately thought, "This isn't fair!" Just then, the professor said, "We didn't talk much about those topics, but they were in the textbook." Michael started feeling queasy as the professor continued. "I told you at the beginning of the semester that you were responsible for all the material in the textbook." Michael's stomach sank into his shoes. He wasn't feeling so smug after all.

> **Grace disturbs our sense of justice.**

The professor instructed the students to keep their

exam papers face down until everyone had received the test. When Michael turned over his test, he was shocked to see that all the blanks were already filled in. Thinking he'd accidentally received the answer key, he then saw a note at the bottom of the test. It read, "This is your final exam. All the answers are correct. You will receive a perfect score on the final exam. The reason you passed this test is because the creator of the test took it for you. All the work you did or didn't do in preparing for the exam did not help you get the A. You have just experienced...grace." Michael learned more about God's grace that day than from any theological lecture. The professor had the right to do what he did because it was his class. God has the right to be as generous as He wants to be! That's not fair, but thank God, that's grace.

> God has the right to be as generous as He wants to be!

Dare Not to Compare

If the workers had received their pay apart from knowing what the others received, they probably would have gone home happy. Someone has said that comparison is toxic to the soul. You may not mind if your neighbors drive a new Lexus, but if you just bought a used Chevrolet Malibu and find out your neighbors paid less for their tricked out Lexus than you did for your Chevy, you're not going to be so happy for them.

Abraham Lincoln recognized the truth of this principle and its widespread effects. He told about walking down the street one day with his two young sons, Tab and Willie. Both boys were howling with displeasure. A friend met him and said, "What's wrong with the boys, Abe?" Lincoln looked at his children and said, "What's wrong with my boys is what's wrong with the world. I have three chestnuts and they both want two."

> **The Bible warns against grumbling (James 5:9).**

The longer you've worked in the vineyard, the greater the temptation to grumble about what you see happening around you. Sadly, the temptation is to grumble when a newbie comes along and experiences God's blessings when you feel you've labored long and hard without a word of thanks. Or when we hear of a death row prisoner who accepts Christ, we may secretly think, "Yeah, right." The Bible warns against grumbling, "Don't grumble against each other, brothers, or you will be judged. The Judge is standing at the door!" (James 5:9).

Can you think of a couple of grumblers in the Bible who complained about grace? Jonah preached to the people of Nineveh that God would destroy them unless they repented. They repented, but Jonah resented God for showing His grace in forgiving them. The conclusion of the parable Jesus told about the prodigal son ends with a vignette featuring his older brother. I preached an entire message once on the "Parable of the Pouting Son." He refused to join the party and complained to his father about the gracious generosity showered on "this son of yours"—he couldn't even bring himself to acknowledge his own flesh and blood.

God has brought all kinds of people into our church over the years. I've had a few people approach me and say, "Pastor, I saw someone last Sunday, and they had tattoos all over their body. I don't like it." Or "Did you see the guy wearing SHORTS to church?" Or "Did you see that gal with all those piercings?" I usually smile and respond, "Well, it's a good thing it's not YOUR church because God loves everyone, and this is HIS church." Instead of being thankful for being saved early in life, we begrudge those who come into the kingdom later. You say, "It's just not fair!"? No, thank God, that's grace.

> **Ask God to help you stop comparing yourself with or grumbling against others.**

So What?

The practical application of this story Jesus told is simple. Because God has been unreasonably generous to you, now you are blessed to be inexplicably generous to others. Ask God to help you stop comparing yourself with or grumbling against others. Instead, pass along the same grace that you received—trust me, they need it just as much (and maybe even more) than you do. That may mean being outrageously kind to someone who has wronged you in the past. That may mean being scandalously generous with someone who has no ability to reciprocate. That may mean letting go of a grudge. You may think in your heart, "Wait, that's not FAIR!" No, thank God, that's grace.

QUESTIONS TO THINK ABOUT

What seemed unfair to you about the way the workers were treated?

What was the attitude of the others who had been working all day in the field?

Why do you think the others reacted that way? Can you relate?

Why is grace so hard to understand?

What is the ultimate reward for a Christian?

How can you demonstrate more grace toward others?

How can you spend some time meditating on and thanking God for grace today?

CHAPTER 7
God's Final Harvest

A Parable about the Existence of Evil

Matthew 13:24-30

At the beginning of the 20th century, most Americans were very optimistic that the world was moving toward Utopia. The evolution of human progress and innovations in travel and industry convinced them that the world as a whole was getting better and better. Then came World War I, the "War to end all Wars," followed by World War II—decimating their Utopian ideals. Those in the 21st century who believe the world is steadily getting better are rare indeed. With the rise of terrorism and global economic problems, instead things seem to be going from bad to worse.

Actually, nearly every generation has been convinced that their world was spiraling out of control. I came across a humorous poem by my favorite author,

Anonymous, that read:

> My granddad, viewing earth's worn cogs, said, "Things are going to the dogs."
>
> His granddad, in his house of logs, said, "Things are going to the dogs."
>
> And his granddad, in the Flemish bogs, said, "Things are going to the dogs."
>
> And his granddad, in his old skin togs, said, "Things are going to the dogs."
>
> But there's one thing I have to state: The dogs have had a good long wait.

Vance Havner once said, "I used to say the world was going to the dogs, but I've stopped saying that out of respect for dogs!" So, which is it? Are things going to get better one day here on earth, or are they going to get worse? First-Century Jews and Gentiles wondered the same question. In explanation of this age-old inquiry, Jesus told a parable:

> God's kingdom is like a farmer who planted good seed in his field. That night, while his hired men were asleep, his enemy sowed thistles all through the wheat and slipped away before dawn. When the first green shoots appeared and the grain began to form, the thistles showed up, too.
>
> The farmhands came to the farmer and said, "Master, that was clean

> seed you planted, wasn't it? Where did these thistles come from?"
>
> He answered, "Some enemy did this."
>
> The farmhands asked, "Should we weed out the thistles?"
>
> He said, "No, if you weed the thistles, you'll pull up the wheat, too. Let them grow together until harvest time. Then I'll instruct the harvesters to pull up the thistles and tie them in bundles for the fire, then gather the wheat and put it in the barn." (***The Message,*** Matthew 13:24-30)

Then Jesus told two additional brief parables back-to-back. Afterwards, He took a break inside a house to let His audience ruminate on what He was teaching them. That's when His disciples came to Him, as they often did, asking Him to explain the parable about the wheat and thistles (weeds). I can imagine the disciples nodding their heads when Jesus had addressed the crowd earlier, as if they perfectly understood all He was saying. But they had no clue! At their first opportunity, they wanted to know what in the world He was talking about. Fortunately for us, the explanation of the cast of characters in this intriguing tale is captured in Matthew 13:37-43:

Are things going to get better, or are they going to get worse?

> So he explained. The farmer who sows the pure seed is the Son of Man. The field is the world, the pure seeds are subjects of the kingdom,

the thistles are subjects of the Devil, and the enemy who sows them is the Devil. The harvest is the end of the age, the curtain of history. The harvest hands are angels.

The picture of thistles pulled up and burned is a scene from the final act. The Son of Man will send his angels, weed out the thistles from his kingdom, pitch them in the trash, and be done with them. They are going to complain to high heaven, but nobody is going to listen. At the same time, ripe, holy lives will mature and adorn the kingdom of their Father.

In the Parable of the Sower, the seeds were the same, but the soils were different.

The Bad Seed

If this parable were made into a movie, there would be three scenes: sowing the seeds, growing the plants and mowing the harvest. Once more, Jesus chooses an agricultural setting to communicate an important truth—something familiar that would make His audience pay attention.

In the story, the farmer planted wheat seeds (like he did in the Parable of the Sower earlier in that same chapter, hoping for a harvest). In the next scene, however, a wicked farmer slipped into the field and planted thistle seeds (weeds)—right on top of what the good farmer had just done. In the Parable of the Sower, the seeds were the same, but the soils were different. Notice that in this parable the soil is the same for both farmers, but the seeds are very different.

Is Everyone God's Child?

I'll never forget the Sunday morning I spoke on being a member of God's family. Some people were surprised because I said, "We are all God's creation—but not everyone is His child." You may hear someone trying to reconcile Christianity with Islam or Buddhism by saying something politically correct like, "We're all God's children." I hope you'll lovingly correct this platitude by explaining that we're all God's creation, but only those who know Jesus are His children. Does that sound narrow-minded? I agree that it doesn't make for a nice bumper sticker. However, according to Jesus, there are only two categories of people.

> **According to Jesus, there are only two categories of people.**

As the wheat began to grow in the farmer's field, so did the weeds. A weed that often infests wheat fields is called darnel, which looks a lot like a wheat crop in the early stages of growth. Wheat farmers in Kansas nicknamed it "cheat." The farmer's servants questioned him about the state of his crops, and he immediately knew what had happened.

God gets the blame for a lot of the evil we see today, but Jesus identifies an enemy in this story who is actively opposing His work in the world. The word He used for "enemy" is from the root word for "hate."

The devil despises God's work and God's people, so He strategizes how to sabotage God's redemptive plan. He does this by "planting" bad people throughout every corner of the earth. Every country has murderers, rapists, robbers and other criminals. The farmer wasted no time identifying who was behind the work when he saw his field littered with thistles. When evil appears, we can immediately know this is the devil's work, not God's.

When evil appears, we can immediately know this is the devil's work, not God's.

Have you noticed how the same people who blame God for evil seldom give Him credit for the good that happens? Years ago, a pastor friend of mine visited a family whose teenage son had been killed in a car accident. The teenager had been drinking and lost control of his car. The boy's family didn't go to church, but one of the neighbors was a member of my friend's church (which is why they asked my friend to do the funeral). After he talked with the devastated parents in their home on the evening of the accident, my friend quietly suggested having a word of prayer together.

The mother burst out, "No! Absolutely not! God killed my son, so there will be no praying in my house!" My friend was shocked, but as he reflected on that experience he realized that was probably the first time

God had crossed her mind in a long time. When her son was born, she probably didn't thank God for his birth. However, when tragedy struck, suddenly God was responsible. The devil must laugh with glee every time God gets blamed for his evil schemes.

Taking the Bad with the Good

When I was a sophomore in high school, our football coach plowed up the field between the hash marks and planted grass seed. One night, a friend and I slipped into the stadium and planted rows of corn seed. As the grass seed started to grow under our coach's careful plan of watering and fertilizing, so did the stalks of corn. Initially, the coach was mad because he thought someone had sold him bad grass seed. Of course, we couldn't keep quiet about our responsibility for what was obviously one of the most successful pranks in my high school's history. We told some of our friends what we'd done and word soon reached our coach!

The devil must laugh with glee every time God gets blamed for his evil schemes.

He made us get on our hands and knees in the hot sun and gingerly pull up every baby corn stalk as he supervised. If we disturbed a single blade of his precious grass, he made us run wind sprints. Trust me, I believe the verse in Galatians 6:7 about reaping whatever you sow. In my case, we had to pull out the corn, but in Jesus' story, the servants were told not to pull up the weeds because it would damage the wheat. The farmer gave the unusual instruction to let both plants grow together. Why? The roots of the darnel (the weeds) were intertwined with the wheat. Pulling out the weeds would threaten the wheat's growth.

Wait a minute. What do weeds and wheat have to do with good people and evil people? Look a little deeper into the story. In this parable, Jesus taught an important truth about the problem of evil. Bad people co-exist among the good people for now—they're in our neighborhoods, our cities and our country. That doesn't mean we should allow criminal activity to thrive. God has given government the power to punish evildoers. Until Jesus returns, He has also called us to be the salt of the earth, spiritual agents that slow down the moral corruption of our world like salt does to decay. We're called to be the light of world in the midst of the moral darkness, but it's not our job as individuals to assume responsibility for "chopping out" all the bad people. Like the anxious farmhands in Jesus' story, our first instinct is to rip out all the weeds. We often wonder when we see the horrific stories on

What do weeds and wheat have to do with good people and evil people?

the evening news, "Why doesn't God take care of all the evil in the world already?" He is. And He will. But when He executes His perfect justice at the final harvest, it will also mark the end of life as we know it. So, for now we wait while evil continues to co-exist much closer to us and much more intertwined with our lives than we would ever want.

The Final Harvest

In 1895, a man named Pearl Wait invented a way to mix fruit syrup with gelatin. His wife called his concoction, Jell-O. After trying to market his Jell-O for a couple of years, he became impatient with the slow sales. He sold the rights to the recipe to his neighbor, Frank Woodward, for $450. By 1905, sales of Jell-O reached $1 million, and General Foods later bought out Mr. Woodward. Because Mr. Wait could not wait, none of his descendants receive a penny of royalty from the sale of 1.1 million boxes of Jell-O sold every day. It's been said that good things come to those who wait. We must wait patiently for the return of Christ and the time of God's final harvest.

We must wait patiently for the return of Christ and the time of God's final harvest.

When the time came for the harvest in this story, the servants eagerly went out to mow down the crop using an ancient farming tool called a hand scythe. As instructed, they cut it all down together. Then they started the process of separating the weeds from the wheat. They bundled the weeds to burn and stored the remaining wheat in sheaves in the farmer's barn.

There are several passages in the Bible that compare the final judgment to a harvest, including Revelation 14. According to the Bible, there are only two eternal destinations. One is heaven, represented by the farmer's barns. The other is hell, represented by the bonfire where the servants tossed the weeds (indicating that the fires of hell are not just symbolic). Although it may not be a popular thing to say today, I am convinced that Jesus taught a literal heaven and a literal hell throughout the New Testament.

There are several passages in the Bible that compare the final judgment to a harvest.

Some people like to say the devil is "alive and well" and living on planet earth. He's alive, but he's not well. Since the cross, he has been fighting a losing battle. The Bible says Jesus came to "destroy" the works of the devil (1 John 3:8). Going back to the beginning of time, God predicted in Genesis 3 that "the serpent" (symbolic of the devil) would strike the heel of the Messiah (at the cross), but that the Messiah would then crush Satan's head. A heel wound isn't fatal, but a crushed head is a fatal blow. Since the cross, Jesus has continued to crush the serpent's head—one day for all eternity. Revelation 20:10 predicts, "And the devil, who deceived them, was thrown into the lake of burning sulfur, where the beast and the false prophet had been thrown. They will be tormented day and night for ever and ever."

You see, hell was never designed for human habitation. Jesus said in Matthew 25:41 that the lake of fire was prepared for the devil and his angels. Satan is like a spiritual suicide bomber. He knows about his final punishment, so he is desperately trying to take as many people with him as he can. The wicked end up in hell because they refuse to accept God's offer of unconditional love and grace. And yet God does not "send" anyone to hell. People send themselves there as a consequence of their own stubborn refusal of God's gift. He is the loving God who is patiently waiting for everyone—even the vilest people among us—to come to Him for salvation (2 Peter 3:9). Don't worry—the devil's fate is already sealed when God puts an end to evil once and for all.

Don't worry—the devil's fate is already sealed when God puts an end to evil once and for all.

Counterfeit Christians

Evil people represent the weeds in this story—we see them everywhere in our world today. But the weeds are also counterfeit Christians—and the devil plants them in our churches. Whenever God creates something, Satan always tries to counterfeit it. The evil farmer in this story planted something that looked so close to the real thing that it was almost indistinguishable. God produces authentic believers through the indwelling of the Holy Spirit. On the other hand, Satan plants counterfeit churchgoers to deceive others about how to be saved. They believe the devil's lie that keeping religious rules and following religious rituals will get a person to heaven. They haven't yet understood that the only people who will make it to heaven are those who have a personal relationship with Jesus.

Satan plants counterfeit churchgoers to deceive others about how to be saved.

Billy Graham once said his greatest mission field has been the rolls of churches. During his crusades, about 70% of the people saved are members of churches somewhere. They are "weeds among the wheat"—good people who probably thought they were already saved. Jesus describes these counterfeit churchgoers with a sobering prediction: "Not everyone who says to me, 'Lord, Lord,' will enter the kingdom of heaven, but only he who does the will of my Father who is in heaven. Many will say to me on that day, 'Lord, Lord, did we not prophesy in your name, and in your name drive out demons and perform many miracles?' Then I will tell them plainly, 'I never knew you. Away from me you evildoers" (Matthew 7:21-23).

These are religious people who walked and talked like believers, and they even knew the right "church" language. They filled their calendars with religious activities, fully expecting to be saved. But Jesus said, "I never KNEW you." In its simplest form, salvation is *knowing* Jesus (John 17:3). It's not enough to know *about* Jesus. I know about George Washington, but I cannot say I know him.

In its simplest form, salvation is *knowing* Jesus.

Years ago when I was a youth evangelist, I was preaching a weekend revival in Alabama. Before the Sunday night service at the church, I had dinner in the home of the chairman of the deacons. As I took a seat in his den, I saw something out of the corner of my eye. Coiled beside me on the floor was a huge rattlesnake, and I jumped straight up in the air! I then quickly realized it was stuffed. And so were the feral hog, several deer heads and bobcat nearby. As it turned out, my host was also a taxidermist.

That evening after my message on the difference between real and counterfeit Christians, I was surprised to see my host walk down the center aisle of the church and lay his head on his pastor's shoulder. They stood talking and praying for several verses of "Just as I Am." Finally, the pastor stopped the song and told the congregation to listen to what this man had to say. The deacon chairman then turned to the congregation and with tears in his eyes confessed he had been a "counterfeit" Christian. Everyone in that church knew he was a taxidermist. His job was making dead animals look alive. He compared his life to one of his stuffed animals—he looked spiritually alive, but he was dead on the inside. He wanted his church to know that he had prayed to receive Christ for the first time that night. Then he turned to his pastor and said, "I feel that I have to resign as a deacon because when I was elected to this position I wasn't even saved." At that, the pastor nodded and said, "Brother, we accept your resignation as a deacon..." The man's face was stone-like with contrition. Then the pastor smiled and said, "...and we rejoice that you are truly saved now." Turning to the congregation he asked, "All

I want you to have the assurance that you are indeed saved.

in favor of restoring our brother as the chairman of the deacons say, 'Amen.'" Thunderous "amens" reverberated throughout that little church.

My purpose in writing about counterfeit Christians is not to make you doubt your salvation. I want you to have the assurance that you are indeed saved. Agriculturally speaking, a wheat farmer can easily tell the difference between wheat and weeds. As the harvest nears, the tops of the wheat stalks bow, heavy with grain. Meanwhile, the grainless weeds stand tall and straight. Likewise, the more mature and fruitful we become as true believers, the more we bow before the Lord in humility. Counterfeit Christians tend to stand tall, proud of their religious accomplishments which they foolishly believe will transport them to heaven. The Bible promises that one day "every knee will bow and every tongue will confess that Jesus is Lord" (Philippians 2:10-11). If you will bow before Jesus today and crown Him as the Lord of your life, you can know beyond a doubt that you are a true believer.

"...every knee will bow and every tongue will confess that Jesus is Lord."

Rash Judgments Can Cause Harm

So, is it our responsibility as true believers to crank up our spiritual weed-eaters and start whacking away to remove the weeds in the Church? Remember the farmer's instruction to the over-anxious servants who wanted to do the same thing when they found out what their enemy had done. He said to wait. The reason we're not qualified as spiritual weed-eaters is because we can't know for certain who is a stalk of wheat and who is a weed. We can look for evidence of the fruit of the Spirit, as the Bible says. Nevertheless, only God knows beyond a doubt who is saved and who is not. Sometimes the weeds and the wheat look the same.

> Only God knows beyond a doubt who is saved and who is not.

Despite our good intentions, pulling out the weeds ourselves (instead of waiting for the final harvest) can do more harm than good in our churches. I've seen gardens that looked as if they were full of weeds, but it turns out they were full of flowers just waiting to bloom. If it had been left up to me, I would have weed-whacked the entire thing. Also being colorblind doesn't help matters! Thankfully, the Father is the expert Gardener in John 15, and He alone can tell the difference without fail.

The unholy desire on the part of Christians to eliminate bad weeds has created some dark episodes in human history. Around the year 1000A.D., the Christians in the Holy Roman Empire decided they should root out the infidels who were occupying the Holy Land. These attempts were called The Crusades. In one of the first Crusades, Christian knights from Western Europe stormed through an Arab town on their way to the Holy Land. They killed everyone with brown skin wearing turbans. It was not until they turned over the bodies that they found crosses around the necks of most of their victims. It never occurred to them that a Christian might have brown skin and wear a turban. While trying to cut down the weeds, they destroyed the beautiful wheat.

At the final harvest, we may be surprised at some of the people who turn up in God's heavenly barnful of wheat instead of the bonfire of hell. We may be tempted to ask, "What are YOU doing here in my barn?" (Of course, it is God's barn, not ours; He determines what goes in it.) By the same token, we may be surprised at some of the people who *aren't* there as well.

We may be tempted to ask, "What are YOU doing here in my barn?"

From Weeds to Wheat

Now, what do you think: Is the world getting better or is it getting worse? According to this parable, the best answer is what Jesus would say, "Both!" It just depends on whether you are one of the weeds or wheat. For the devil's weeds, the world is going to get worse—a lot worse. Yet for the stalks of God's wheat, the future is as bright as the brilliant sun shining on the field.

There is a point at which all metaphors and parables break down, including this one, since the kingdom of heaven is actually about people, not plants. That's why Jesus introduced a series of parables like this one by making a comparison, saying, "God's kingdom is *like...*" People and plants have an entirely different make-up. From a purely agricultural perspective, a weed, is a weed, is a weed; it can never become a stalk of wheat. In His grace, however, Jesus can dramatically transform a spiritual weed into something it never was before: a vibrant stalk of God's wheat, heavy with grain to share with others who need to know Christ. That's the miracle of salvation. No wonder the Bible says, "If anyone is in Christ, he is a new creation" (2 Corinthians 5:17).

QUESTIONS TO THINK ABOUT

Is the world getting better or worse? Explain.

Is every person a child of God? What is the difference between being God's creation and His child?

In this story, who sowed the "bad seed"? What did this parable teach you about the devil's strategies?

How does the existence of evil in the world today perplex you?

What did the servants in this story want to do when they saw the weeds growing?

Why are rash judgments about people's character, especially in a church, dangerous?

How does the knowledge of a global "final harvest" motivate you to share your faith?

CHAPTER 8
Here Comes the Bridegroom!

The Parable of the Sleepy Bridesmaids
Matthew 25:1-13

In 40 years of pastoring, I have performed several hundred weddings. I've never counted them, but I'm sure it's somewhere close to 1000 by now. Everybody loves a wedding! I once heard about a lady who married a banker. Unfortunately, he soon died, so she married an actor—but he died, too. For her third marriage, she chose a preacher. Sadly, he died, too. Finally, she married a mortician. When somebody asked her about her four weddings she explained, "It wasn't by accident that I married a banker, an actor, a preacher and a mortician. I planned it that way: one for the money, two for the show, three to get ready and four to go!"

In our Western culture, a wedding ceremony is all about the bride. In the typical ceremony, the groom and the preacher walk in together. Then the bridesmaids and groomsmen take their places on alternate sides. Some families include kids to serve as flower girls or ring bearers, which can make for an interesting wedding. One little guy came down the aisle holding the pillow with the rings, growling as he walked along. Afterwards, his mother scolded him for making noise in the wedding. "But Mom," he said, "you told me I was the ring bear."

In our Western culture, a wedding ceremony is all about the bride.

When the bride's mother stands and the music plays, it's a cue for everyone else to stand as the back door opens and the bride enters the room. Every eye is on the bride as she walks down the aisle, except mine. I prefer to watch the groom as he smiles in anticipation, watching his bride slowly approach him.

As kids, we sang funny songs to the tune of "Here Comes the Bride" about the bride being big, fat and wide (and the groom skinny as a broom). However, you're probably not surprised that those aren't the original lyrics. Actually, the words "Here Comes the Bride" aren't part of Wagner's composition at all. The chorus is from his opera *Lohengrin*, written in German in 1850. The first line translates as: "Faithfully guided, draw near to where the blessing of love shall preserve you." The theme song of Jesus' parables about a wedding is: "Here Comes the Bridegroom!" He brought the attention solely on the bridegroom—which was an accurate portrayal of the focus in a Jewish wedding.

The setting where he told this wedding story was anything but festive—only a few hours away from Jesus' arrest. He could have taught on any topic, knowing it would be one of His final teachings before the cross. He chose a wedding to talk about His return.

> **Jesus brought the attention solely on the bridegroom.**

In this chapter, He repeats a pattern several times. Whenever you see the same biblical statement repeated in a passage, pay attention. For instance, in Matthew 24:36 He says about His return, "No one knows about that day or hour, not even the angels in heaven, nor the Son, but only the Father." A few verses later, He adds, "Therefore keep watch, because you do not know on what day your Lord will come (v42)." Add to that v44: "So you also must be ready, because the Son of Man will come at an hour when you do not expect him." We know to ignore the manmade chapter division between Matthew 24 and 25 because He continues the thread of being ready: "Therefore keep watch, because you do not know the day or the hour" (25:13). Is He trying to tell us something? In case we didn't get it, the Great Storyteller begins His tale this way:

> God's kingdom is like ten young virgins who took oil lamps and went out to greet the bridegroom. Five were silly and five were smart. The silly virgins took lamps, but no extra oil. The smart virgins took jars of oil to feed their lamps. The bridegroom didn't show up when they expected him, and they all fell asleep.
>
> In the middle of the night someone yelled out, "He's here! The bridegroom's here! Go out and greet him!"
>
> The ten virgins got up and got their lamps ready. The silly virgins said to the smart ones, "Our lamps are going out; lend us some of your oil."
>
> They answered, "There might not be enough to go around; go buy your own."
>
> They did, but while they were out buying oil, the bridegroom arrived. When everyone who was there to greet him had gone into the wedding feast, the door was locked.
>
> Much later, the other virgins, the silly ones, showed up and knocked on the door, saying, "Master, we're here. Let us in."
>
> He answered, "Do I know you? I don't think I know you."
>
> So stay alert. You have no idea when he might arrive.
>
> (***The Message,*** Matthew 25:1-13)

"So stay alert. You have no idea when he might arrive."

A Jewish Wedding

In Western culture, a wedding has two stages: the engagement and the wedding ceremony itself. Compare that to traditional Jewish culture's three separate wedding phases. First, came the "arrangement stage," where the parents of the son and daughter make a formal agreement, including a dowry, between the families. Unlike our Western culture, the groom's family paid all the wedding expenses. (Having paid for two daughters to get married, I favor the Jewish custom of letting the groom's family pay for the wedding!) This arrangement stage often took place when the bride and groom were merely children. They had no choice in the matter. Sometimes I think many American parents today would be in favor of choosing their kids' spouses—and some even give it a go!

A betrothal could last almost a year while the groom was preparing a place at his father's house...

The second step in the Jewish wedding was the betrothal. In this ceremony, the bride and groom exchanged vows before their family members. The marriage would be official at this point, but the newlyweds did not live together, and there was no physical contact. A betrothal could last almost a year while the groom was preparing a place at his father's house for the couple to live. Sound familiar? Jesus said that in His Father's house were many rooms where He was going to prepare a place for us.

The third stage of a Jewish wedding provides the setting of this parable: the wedding feast. The bride would still be living in her parents' house at this point. At an unexpected time, her groom would swoop in to claim her one day and take her to his father's house for the celebration. This was a joyous experience for the bride and groom and their friends. The bride wouldn't know the exact time the groom would come for her, so she had to stay ready. She posted bridesmaids outside her house to keep watch for him, giving her a few minutes' warning that he was on his way. The groom and his friends, however, would make a game of sneaking in undetected and taking the bride. At the sight of the bridegroom, someone would announce, "Here comes the bridegroom!" Once the groom claimed his bride, the eager bridesmaids would walk in a procession on either side of the couple, lamps held high, all the way to his father's house.

> **The bride posted bridesmaids outside her house to keep watch for the bridegroom.**

One interpretation of this parable assigns the cast of characters this way. The Bride is the Church, Jesus is the Bridegroom and one day He's going to claim His Bride unannounced and take the Church to His Father's house in heaven. I could write an entire chapter on that truth. Something's missing in that interpretation for this story, though. Where is the bride mentioned in this parable? She isn't there. Even the bridegroom plays a minor role. Instead, Jesus highlights the slumbering bridesmaids. Who are they? These bridesmaids represent people in the Church who are instructed to watch for the return of Christ.

Ready or Not, Here He Comes

The lamps Jesus described were common small lamps with a wick made of cloth soaked in olive oil. The bridesmaids in this story had matching invitations to the wedding, identical roles to play, and each one carried a lamp for the procession. But only half the girls were truly prepared for a wedding. Each had fixed her hair, slipped on some heels and applied some lip gloss, but half of them neglected the single most important requirement for their job—oil for the lamps.

In the Old Testament, oil is a symbol of the Holy Spirit.

In the Old Testament, oil is a symbol of the Holy Spirit. The prophet Zechariah describes a vision of two huge olive trees dripping oil into bowls and writes, "Not by might nor by power, but by my Spirit, says the Lord Almighty" (Zechariah 4:6). The five "silly" girls represent people who appear religious but lack the one quality that distinguishes a true believer. They have all the outward trappings of faith. They attend church, they read their Bibles and they help old people across the street—but the Holy Spirit does not indwell them.

A pastor friend of mine in Houston told about having a fashion emergency one Saturday when he discovered his suit needed to be dry-cleaned for a wedding he was doing that night. Fortunately, he remembered a store that advertised "One-Hour Dry Cleaning." Unfortunately, the store was on the other side of Houston. When he arrived after a long drive, he dropped off the suit and said he would be back in about an hour to pick it up. "Oh," the clerk said casually. "This suit won't be ready until Tuesday." Confused, my friend said, "I thought you did dry-cleaning in an hour." She just chuckled and said, "Oh, no. That's just the name of the store. We don't actually do that."

Some people are Christians in name only.

Some people are Christians in name only. They claim to be Christians, but they're guilty of false advertising. They do a lot of good things, but they never get around to doing the best thing. Here are three examples:

Going to church is good; coming to Christ is better

You can have your own pew or seat staked out, and you can have perfect attendance for a year. However, if all you have ever done is come to church, and you've never come to Christ, then you are no better than a foolish bridesmaid who misses the wedding.

Being baptized is good; being born again is better

You can be baptized so many times in a farm pond until you know every catfish by its first name, and you still might not be saved. The water of baptism doesn't wash away your sins. Only the blood of Jesus can do that. Jesus told Nicodemus, a morally religious man, he had to be "born again" (John 3).

> **Going to church is good; coming to Christ is better.**

Giving money is good; giving your heart to Jesus is better

If you hear Jesus knocking at the door of your heart, don't slide a $20 bill under the door. God doesn't need your money. He wants to have a personal relationship with you. One way to know if you're truly saved is to check your heart. Do you have a longing for and an excitement about Jesus coming back? Or is it just another religious doctrine that you think about every now and then?

Something Borrowed, Something Blue

Many brides who dress for their wedding day follow a wives' tale by wearing "something old, something new; something borrowed, something blue." In God's wedding between His Son and the Church, there will be nothing borrowed. You cannot borrow someone else's faith—you must express your own. In Jesus' parable, all the bridesmaids awoke from their slumber and trimmed their lamps. The foolish ones' wicks sputtered and flickered, but they could not burn because they were out of oil. They tried to solve their problem by borrowing oil from the others, but that would not leave enough for those girls to complete the procession either.

> In God's wedding between His Son and the Church, there will be nothing borrowed.

Why does Jesus include this interesting dialogue between the girls? I think it emphasizes the fact that you cannot borrow another person's faith if you don't have any. For example, you can learn from your parents' faith, but you can't use their faith as your own. Even though your spouse may be saved, he or she cannot become your savior. Those who have received the grace of God can't impart that gift to anyone else. But that doesn't mean some people won't try it!

Through the years, I've seen people try to ride into heaven on granddaddy's coattails because he happened to be the preacher at First Ebenezer Baptist Church. God has children, but He has no grandchildren. The spiritual influences in your life can instill God's Word in your heart and train you in the things of God, but they can't give you their faith. You have to be prepared for Christ's return on your own.

A Surprise Ending

The forgetful girls headed off, but where would they be able to buy oil at midnight? There were no 24-hour Hebrew-Marts. What was the plan? I don't think there was one. I think they knew the gig was up—they would miss the procession for sure. However, I imagine they planned all along to grovel at the door later, thinking they would be let inside at the last minute. Sadly, that is many people's backup plan for getting into heaven. They can't imagine that God will not let them inside if they ask nicely or give a really good excuse.

The spiritual influences in your life can't give you their faith.

But this parable has a surprise ending.

Try to picture it. The five girls show up panting for breath from running all that way, holding their high heels and trying to smooth down their frazzled hair. "We're here!" they cry in a singsong voice. "Sorry we're late!" If we were telling this story, the groom would swing open the door, the crowd inside would roar with excitement and they would all join the party.

In Jesus' version of the story, the girls called the groom "Master" or "Sir, Sir" in the NIV translation. These are the same familiar words: "Lord, Lord" in Matthew 7 where Jesus said, "Not everyone who says to me, 'Lord, Lord' will enter the Kingdom of heaven, but only he who does the will of my Father who is in heaven." The groom's response in Jesus' story is an echo of v23 where Jesus predicts, "Then I will tell them plainly, 'I never knew you. Away from me, you evil doers.'" The bridegroom in Jesus' story responds with the same blank stare at the girls, as if he never knew them at all. Bridesmaids are supposed to be the bride's most intimate friends. We have to doubt the sincerity of the girls' friendship with the bride if they were that callous with the wedding preparations. In truth, they could not have cared less about the wedding.

The Bible speaks about the prevalence of self-deception.

I've heard people say, "You can fool everybody else, but you can't fool yourself." Oh, yes, you can. The Bible speaks about the prevalence of self-deception. Jeremiah notes that the "heart is deceitful above all things" (17:9). It's possible to deceive yourself into thinking you are a real Christian, when you have merely grown comfortable acting like a Christian.

AAA Auto Club reports answering 500,000 calls a year from people who run out of gas. In the past, gas gauges weren't that accurate, so it wasn't that hard to run out of gas. Today's vehicles are equipped with lights, bell tones and even pleasant electronic female voices to warn us we're running low on fuel. It's kind of inexcusable to run out of gas these days! But if you've ever been one of the unfortunate ones to do so, you know exactly how it happens regardless of the warnings. You know full well how you can deceive yourself into thinking you've still got enough gas in the tank to keep going. *Just one more errand. One more mile.* However, for millions of drivers, the power of positive thinking results in a cough, a shudder and a car on the side of the road. When it comes to salvation, the page you're reading is another warning light. Are you ignoring it? Or will you do something about it?

> **The door of heaven is open right now, but one day it will be shut...**

You see, the door of heaven is open right now, but one day the door will be shut and no amount of pleading will open it. It will be too late. A few years ago, I was making a flight connection at the Dallas airport to fly to another major city. My first flight was late arriving, so I had to run to my next gate. As I reached the boarding area, I breathed a sigh of relief because I could see the plane was still parked at the gate. I approached the gate agent with my boarding pass, but she informed me, "I'm sorry, you can't get on this flight. Boarding is over."

I pointed through the window to the plane and said, "But I can see the plane right there. It hasn't left yet!" She smiled sweetly as if she hadn't heard me at all and said, "Sorry, but FAA regulations say once the door is shut, no one is allowed on the aircraft." (I've since learned the airlines often make an exception to this rule, but my gate agent friend wasn't going to budge.) In total frustration, I watched my plane push back and taxi out to the runway. Someone said opportunity only knocks once—but by the time you unlatch the chain, unlock two dead bolts and turn off the alarm, opportunity has already gone. Today is just one more door of opportunity for you to give your life to Christ. One day, the door will be shut and you don't want to be left standing on the wrong side of that door.

Today is just one more door of opportunity for you to give your life to Christ.

At the Midnight Hour

In the mid 1800s, a man named Elisha worked tirelessly on an invention with the potential to change the entire world. In repeated tests, the device worked perfectly. For some reason, he delayed filling out the paperwork for the patent for two months. When he finally arrived at the U.S. Patent Office, he was devastated to learn that only two hours earlier that morning a schoolteacher who had been conducting similar experiments had filed for a patent. That teacher's name? Bell. Alexander Graham Bell. The invention? A device to transmit a human voice over telegraph wires, the precursor to the telephone. If Elisha Gray had not delayed, Gray Telephone would have taken its place in history instead of Bell Telephone. One man was wise and seized the opportunity when he could. The other man was foolish and waited until it was too late.

> **When Jesus returns there will be a sound of a trumpet and a shout of the archangel.**

According to the Apostle Paul in 1 Thessalonians, when Jesus returns there will be a sound of a trumpet and a shout of the archangel. We don't know who will blow the horn (no, the Bible never says it's Gabriel). However, we do know who will be doing the shouting, since only one archangel is identified in Scripture: Michael. What do you think archangel Michael will shout? No one can know for certain, but I wouldn't be surprised to hear these words reverberate across the expanse of sky, "HERE...COMES...THE BRIDEGROOM!" Will you be ready to meet Him?

QUESTIONS TO THINK ABOUT

Why do you think Jesus chose a wedding to describe His return?

What did you like best about the description of the Jewish wedding tradition?

What distinguished the 5 foolish bridesmaids from the 5 wise ones?

Why did the groom say he didn't know his wife's supposedly best friends?

In what ways do people erroneously assume they have "all the time in the world" to respond to Christ?

What excites you about Jesus' return? What makes you nervous (if anything)?

Are you ready for His return? Why or why not?

CHAPTER 9
Whatcha Gonna Do with Whatcha Got?

A Parable about Potential
Matthew 25:14-30

If I conducted a poll about the most popular parable Jesus ever told, I suspect most people would vote for the Parable of the Prodigal Son. If I polled pastors about the most *practical* parable Jesus ever told, I believe most Christian leaders would vote for this one, often called The Parable of the Talents. I call it the Parable of the Three Managers because it's a parable about managing potential.

Around the turn of the 20th century, Martha Berry had a passion to teach and train poor children in northern Georgia who had no access to education. She had no books, no building and no money—just a dream. She started teaching Sunday school to children in an abandoned church in Possum Trot, Georgia. Her weekly class soon became a daily class. She later opened a boarding school for boys—and though she only had five boarders, she met a need and saw the potential for more.

The school was struggling for money, so Martha Berry often spoke with donors about her cause. In a courageous move, the story is told that she once traveled to Detroit to ask multi-millionaire Henry Ford to make a donation to expand her school. She boldly asked him to donate $1 million, which the multi-millionaire could have afforded. Henry Ford, tired of listening to what seemed like constant requests for money from strangers, reached into his pocket and said, "Here's a dime. That's all the money I have in my pocket, but you can have it." Martha Berry could have been insulted, discouraged and quit. Instead, she used Ford's dime to buy seeds to plant a peanut crop and used that first harvest to plant more peanuts. Martha Berry faithfully sent Henry Ford detailed accountings of each year's harvest. Ford was so impressed that

> **Martha Berry had no books, no building and no money—just a dream.**

he finally visited the Berry School and eventually donated $1 million and then some. He also built the Ford Buildings on campus, a cluster of Gothic-style architecture. Martha Berry died in 1942, but because of her good management, Berry College near Rome, Georgia is now a private four-year college with 1,700 students enrolled. It has the largest campus of any college in the world at 28,000 acres. The Ford Foundation recently gave Berry College a $9.4 million grant, the culmination of a dime into a dream.

In one of my favorite Dennis the Menace cartoons, Dennis and his parents are leaving church as the pastor is standing at the back door. Dennis turns to the pastor in front of the other worshippers and asks loudly, "Now, Pastor what are you going to do with that dollar my dad gave you this morning?" That's funny, but it's actually a pretty good question. In fact, a question worth asking yourself is: "What am I doing with what I've been given?" Jesus told a story to help us answer that question:

> **"What am I doing with what I've been given?"**

> [God's kingdom] is also like a man going off on an extended trip. He called his servants together and delegated responsibilities. To one he gave five thousand dollars, to another two thousand, to a third one thousand,

depending on their abilities. Then he left. Right off, the first servant went to work and doubled his master's investment. The second did the same. But the man with the single thousand dug a hole and carefully buried his master's money.

After a long absence, the master of those three servants came back and settled up with them. The one given five thousand dollars showed him how he had doubled his investment. His master commended him: "Good work! You did your job well. From now on be my partner."

The servant with the two thousand showed how he also had doubled his master's investment. His master commended him: "Good work! You did your job well. From now on be my partner."

The servant given one thousand said, "Master, I know you have high standards and hate careless ways, that you demand the best and make no allowances for error. I was afraid I might disappoint you, so I found a good hiding place and secured your money. Here it is, safe and sound down to the last cent."

> "Get rid of this 'play-it-safe' who won't go out on a limb."

The master was furious. "That's a terrible way to live! It's criminal to live cautiously like that! If you knew I was after the best, why did you do less than the least? The least you could have done would have been to invest the sum with the bankers, where at least I would have gotten a little interest. Take the thousand and give it to the one who risked the most. And get rid of this 'play-it-safe' who won't go out on a limb. Throw him out into utter darkness."

(***The Message,*** Matthew 25:14-30)

Jesus didn't name the three managers, but for the sake of illustration, let's call them Tom, Dick and Harry. Their boss told them he was going away so he left them some funds to manage while he was gone. He gave Tom five coins, Dick two coins and he gave Harry one coin. The master wasn't a socialist; he didn't give each one the same amount because he knew they had different abilities. They were given an amount reflecting their potential.

The master took off on his journey, and the servants went to work. We don't know exactly what they did, but let's imagine Tom took his five coins and started looking for ways to invest it. He noticed how people crossing the Jordan River had to walk 10 miles out of their way to find a place shallow enough to cross, so Tom used the money to buy materials to build a large wood raft for a ferry service. Eventually, he doubled his boss's money. Dick took his two coins and bought a young goat to sell its milk. When the goat was fully grown, Dick sold it for twice the amount he paid for it. Harry, on the other hand, was afraid of losing the money. So he dug a hole and hid the coin. He was a play-it-safe kind of guy.

They were given an amount reflecting their potential.

In the NIV translation, the word for the amount

of money each receives is a "talent," thus this story became known as the "Parable of the Talents." A talent was a certain weight of coins. Some commentators suggest each talent was worth anywhere from $1000 to $100,000. In *The Message,* Eugene Peterson paraphrased it as $1000. Either way, the master placed a lot of trust in his servants to give them a large amount of money to manage.

As a child, I thought that the "parable of the talents" was about talent, not money. Susan Boyle singing on "Britain's Got Talent"—that's talent. Or Dirk Nowitzki shooting his fade-away jump shot—that's talent. I thought the point of this parable was that God gave some people more talent than others. Now that I'm older, I realize the parable is specifically about money, but the general application is much broader than that. It is about managing ALL the resources God has given you—and that includes your special talents. (So, I wasn't that far off as a young child!) In addition to money, God has given each of us a measure of health, time, energy, abilities, influence, relationships, etc. Don't mistake the story Jesus told as just being about money management; it's about life management.

The parable is specifically about money, but the general application is much broader than that.

God Owns it All

It all starts with acknowledging that *everything* I have is a gift from God. I don't own it; I just manage it. The Bible clearly teaches that God is the One who owns it all! Here is a sampling of verses that prove this point:

> "To the Lord your God belong the heavens, even the highest heavens, the earth and everything in it" (Deuteronomy 10:14).

> "For every animal of the forest is mine, and the cattle on a thousand hills" (Psalm 50:10).

> "The world is mine, and all that is in it" (Psalm 50:12).

> "'The silver is mine and the gold is mine,' declares the Lord Almighty" (Haggai 2:8).

The Bible clearly teaches that God is the One who owns it all!

As I was writing this chapter in my study at home, I asked myself if I really believed God owns everything. I decided to proclaim this truth to myself, so I looked around and said aloud, "I'm in God's house, sitting in God's chair. I'm looking out God's window at God's trees and God's garden. I'm wearing God's clothes, and I'm using God's brains and God's hands to type God's words on God's keyboard on God's computer. Later, I'm going to get into God's car and drive on God's roads to visit with some of

God's people." It was actually freeing to say it out loud. Why don't you try it? Here's an affirmation for you to read aloud: "I woke up this morning in God's house! I ate God's food for breakfast. I used God's soap to clean up! I'm breathing God's air. I don't own a thing. God owns it all!" Do you believe that? Here's a test. Let's say you work at a job where you got paid $1000 last week. How much of that $1000 belongs to God? If you said, "Ten percent or $100 belongs to God," then I haven't done a very good job so far in this chapter. But if you thought, "All of it belongs to God," you gave the right answer! This is the starting point for understanding one of the underlying truths behind this parable.

> **One day, we're going to stand before the Lord and give an account for how we managed our resources.**

Facing a Divine Audit

Jesus said the master returned "after a long absence," and it was time to settle accounts. From our time-bound perspective, Jesus has been gone for a long time since He walked the shores of Galilee 2000 years ago. However, His return is closer today than it was yesterday. One day, we're going to stand before the Lord and give an account for how we managed the resources He gave us. The Bible says, "So then, each of us will give an account of himself to God" (Romans 14:12).

In this chapter, I've purposely resisted using the word "stewardship" because when people hear it they think only about giving money to God. I've chosen to use the word "management." That being said, how you manage God's money is indeed a great indicator of how you manage His other resources. Ron Blue, a financial consultant, has written over 20 books on personal financial management from a biblical perspective. He wrote, "You can't fake stewardship. Your checkbook (credit card statement) reveals all that you really believe about stewardship. Your checkbook reflects your goals, priorities, convictions, relationships and even the use of your time. A person who has been a Christian even for a short while can fake prayer, Bible study, evangelism, and going to church and so on but he can't fake what his checkbook reveals" (*The New Master Your Money*, p.23).

> **How you manage God's money is a great indicator of how you manage His other resources.**

Nobody wants to be audited by the IRS. It's a hassle to produce all your tax returns, cancelled checks and bank statements. The IRS requires this information in order to create a money trail of how much money you earned and how much tax you owe. An audit doesn't have to be a scary thing, unless you haven't paid your taxes. I've even heard of the IRS discovering people had overpaid their taxes. Tom and Dick enjoyed reporting to the master about their efforts. But Harry's audit wasn't much fun.

Harry used 37 words to explain why he did nothing. He blamed his failure on the master's hard character:

> "Master," he said, "I knew that you are a hard man, harvesting where you have not sown and gathering where you have not scattered seed. So I was afraid and went out and hid your talent in the ground. See, here is what belongs to you." (NIV)

> **"I was afraid and went out and hid your talent in the ground."**

What kind of person harvests where they don't plant? Think about it: Only a dishonest cheat does that. It was an insult! If Harry had been asked to describe his master, he would have snorted and said, "He's one lazy man. He doesn't even do his own work. He tries to get everyone to do his work for him—then he keeps all the profits for himself." The lazy servant allowed his personal opinion of his boss to justify his failure. Have you noticed how when some people fail, it's never their fault? It's always someone else's fault?

We know Harry's opinion was biased because Tom and Dick considered their master to be a good businessman who knew how to invest money for a good return. Therefore, they followed his example and turned their potential into profit. To which their master said, "Well done, good and faithful servant" (25:21, 23). If Tom and Dick had been asked to describe their master, they would likely use similar language and say, "He's a good and faithful man."

A.W. Tozer wrote: "What we think about God is the most important thing about us." If we view God as a tyrant, we will assume that He doesn't want us to be happy. So, guess what? We become unhappy, paranoid people. Preconceived notions about God's character and His motives prevent people from seeing Him as a God of grace. When we misconstrue God, we end up burying our blessings like the servant in this parable did—afraid we won't measure up to His standards.

If you find you have a skewed view of God, you can always change your opinion.

If you find you have a skewed view of God, you can always change your opinion. And when you do, it changes your life. A few nights ago, I watched the wonderful movie *Shenandoah* again. Jimmy Stewart plays a Virginia farmer named Charlie Anderson who tries to keep his family together during the Civil War. He never attended church, but his deceased wife wanted the children to be raised as Christians. So, Jimmy Stewart attempts to pray this prayer before the meal: "Lord, we cleared this land.

We plowed it, sowed it and harvested it. We cooked the harvest. It wouldn't be here and we wouldn't be eating it if we hadn't done it all ourselves. We worked dog-bone hard for every crumb and morsel, but we thank you Lord just the same for the food we're about to eat. Amen." He didn't have much use for God.

However, in the last scene of the movie, Charlie breaks down and ends his private battle with God. He has lost several of his children by now, and he assumes his youngest son, whom he called "the boy," has also died in the war. To everyone's surprise, Charlie loads up the remaining family members to attend church. When he walks into the church and settles into a pew, the preacher is so surprised he almost has a heart attack. As Charlie stands there without singing, the back door of the church suddenly opens and "the boy" comes limping in. Charlie embraces his son, and the movie ends with everyone singing the Doxology. Man, if that doesn't make you cry, nothing will!

Our potential is God's gift to us.

If you see God as a loving Father, full of grace and truth, then you will try to make the most of the gifts and resources He has given you. If you think everything good in your life came as a result of your own efforts, you won't feel like you owe God anything. Zig Ziglar, one of the most positive Christians I've ever been around, once wrote, "Our potential is God's gift to us. What we do with it is our gift to Him. You are the only person on earth who can use your ability."

Whatcha Gonna Do?

When the master praised Tom and Dick, he issued an invitation for them to become his partner. Fred Smith is a personal friend and a leader at my church. He is one of our Bible Study teachers, and he is the President of the Fourth Partner Foundation. They assist educational, charitable and non-profit organizations in East Texas. There's an interesting story about how the Fourth Partner Foundation got its name. Let me read Fred's explanation: "I was teaching [this parable about the three managers] to a Sunday School class and asked them what would make for a better ending if the Master went away a second time? I proposed a second trip where he left a fourth servant. This servant did not work for the other three and they did not work for him. His role was not to manage or direct but to get a better return for the Master...and a happier ending for the story. That's how I've seen my role in the community." And that's how the Fourth Partner Foundation was born.

"You are the only person on earth who can use your ability."

It's also how I see the role of a church—as a fourth partner, coming alongside Christians to help earn a better return on the Master's investment in each one of them. The church can show you the key to fruitful life management. It's found in verse 16 of the parable when Tom and Dick went "right off to work." In other words, they immediately started developing their potential and kept on working until the master returned. Churches can connect believers with endless opportunities to invest their abilities, time and resources that will fulfill their potential and make a difference in the world—all to God's glory.

God's resources are never to be stored, hoarded or hidden; they are to be put in circulation.

God's resources are never to be stored, hoarded or hidden; they are to be put in circulation. Notice that Tom and Dick had to spend the talents before they received a return. Why hold back what God has given you? What are you waiting for?

Something that has discouraged me through the years is when I see people retiring from serving the Lord. I think retirement from a career or business is a good thing, but I don't find anything in the Word about retiring from serving the Lord. Sometimes we start out serving God with the enthusiasm of Tom and Dick, and then we end up like Peter. We Peter out! What is the consequence of burying our potential because we become too busy or talk ourselves into letting someone else take our place in ministry? The price for burying our potential is steep. Jesus took the one talent away from the lazy servant and gave it to the one with ten. It's the "use it or lose it" principle. If you don't utilize God's resources, don't be surprised when you start to lose them. Relationships, resources, influence and opportunities are all like a muscle—if you don't keep exercising, your muscles will atrophy. How are you flexing your God-given potential in your job, church or community today? Who is becoming part of the kingdom because of your influence? What part of your community is being redeemed on your watch?

Who is becoming part of the kingdom because of your influence?

In 1996, Billy Graham was awarded the Congressional Gold Medal for his service to America. When he was being interviewed afterward by Diane Sawyer he said, "I am humbled by this award. But the only recognition I am looking forward to is when I stand before the Lord Jesus Christ. My greatest reward will be to hear Him say, 'Well done, good and faithful servant.'" Few people have had the opportunities (or the gifting from God) that Billy Graham has had. Yet God calls each of us to do our part to the best of our ability—we're all looking for the same praise from the Master. If God looked at what you've produced so far with the potential He gave you, would He say: "Well done!"? Or would He say you've buried your potential and hand you a shovel to start digging? Now is the time to start using all the potential He gave you while there is still time to make a difference. So, I ask you: Whatcha gonna do with whatcha got?

QUESTIONS TO THINK ABOUT

What do you think is Jesus' most popular parable? Which one is your favorite and why?

In what ways have you expanded your potential the older you get?

How did the three men in this story differ in their attitudes?

How does it help to think of yourself as a "manager" instead of the owner of all you have?

What surprised you most about the harsh reply from the master to the last servant?

Where are you currently using your abilities and talents for God's kingdom?

What talents and abilities have you "buried" out of fear of failure or uncertainty of how to use them for God's purpose?

CHAPTER 10
P.U.S.H. Pray Until Something Happens

The Parable of the Persistent Pray-er
Luke 18:1-8

A young man went into a drugstore to buy three boxes of chocolate: small, medium and large. When the pharmacist asked him about the three boxes, he said, "Well, I'm going over to a new girlfriend's house for supper. Then we're going out. If she only lets me hold her hand, then I'll give her the small box. If she lets me kiss her on the cheek, then I'll give her the medium box. But if she really lets me smooch seriously, I'll give her the big box." He made his purchase and left.

That evening as he sat down at dinner with his girlfriend's family, he asked if he could say the prayer before the meal. He began to pray for almost five minutes. When he finished, his girlfriend leaned over and said, "You never told me you were such a religious person." He whispered back through gritted teeth, "And *you* never told me your dad was a pharmacist!"

Jesus had a great deal to say about prayer. Of everything His disciples watched Him do over the course of three years in ministry, observing how He prayed caught their attention. So, they asked Him one day, "Lord, teach us how to pray." They never asked, "Teach us how to do miracles, or to teach, or to love people." They wanted to emulate His prayer relationship with His Father.

Jesus had a great deal to say about prayer.

In Luke 18:1-8, Jesus shared an intriguing story that from the outset doesn't seem to be about prayer (or anything spiritual) at all. The story begins with a widow and an adversary who was trying to take advantage of her. It's likely someone was trying to cheat her out of some money or land her husband left her. This underhanded dealing was prevalent in Bible times because women had few legal rights. In the Old Testament story of Ruth, she and Naomi returned to Bethlehem as widows with no legal right to claim the land that had belonged to their husbands. Fortunately, when Boaz married Ruth he was able to redeem the land (and Ruth!).

Were it not for the explanation prefacing the parable, the average listener hearing Jesus' story might not have made the connection between prayer and persistence. See what you think when you read the story for yourself:

> Jesus told them a story showing that it was necessary for them to pray consistently and never quit.
>
> There was once a judge in some city who never gave God a thought and cared nothing for people. A widow in that city kept after him: "My rights are being violated. Protect me!"
>
> He never gave her the time of day. But after this went on and on he said to himself, "I care nothing what God thinks, even less what people think. But because this widow won't quit badgering me, I'd better do something and see that she gets justice—otherwise I'm going to end up beaten black-and-blue by her pounding."
>
> Do you hear what that judge, corrupt as he is, is saying? So what makes you think God won't step in and work justice for his chosen people, who continue to cry out for help? Won't he stick up for them? I assure you, he will. He will not drag his feet. But how much of that kind of persistent faith will the Son of Man find on the earth when he returns? (***The Message,*** Luke 18:1-8)

"...What makes you think God won't step in and work justice for his chosen people...?"

In Jesus' parable, this widow faced a terrible judge who didn't have any fear of God (nor did he care what other people thought about him). He was probably a Gentile judge designated by the Roman authorities. His was a legal position that was often bought and sold for selfish gain. The judge himself could make a good living from bribes alone. Our widow had no money to bribe this wicked judge, so her only recourse was to wield her persistent personality like a Samurai warrior. After he dismissed her claim, she kept coming back, constantly begging him for justice. When he heard her voice outside the court, he must have thought, "Oh, no, not *her* again!" In fact, the word He uses to describe her badgering means to "poke in the eye"! The judge was upset because she was constantly in his face, but her persistence paid off when he eventually ruled in her favor.

One of the points Jesus made in this story is the power of persistence.

Don't Worry, Pray

One of the points Jesus made in this story is the power of persistence. Jesus said we ought always to pray and not to give up. A lot of us quit praying about a concern, which creates a vacuum that worry will readily fill. That's exactly what the Greek word translated as *quit* or *give up (enkenkao)* literally means. It means to "be filled with bad thoughts." Worry fills your mind with the worst that could happen. Worry is like water. It begins as a trickle of doubt that creeps into your mind. If it isn't stopped, it soon becomes a stream of fear, which creates a pond of paranoia, which overflows into a river of distress, which develops into a raging torrent of tension. Before you know it, the flood of worry carves a Grand Canyon of anxiety in your mind!

In the parable, the widow didn't sit at home wringing her hands about her problem. Instead of worrying, she got up and approached the only person who could help her.

William Ward, an inspirational author, wrote, "Worry is wasting today's time to clutter up tomorrow's opportunities with yesterday's troubles." Worry is like rocking in a rocking chair—it gives you something to do, but you never go anywhere. The Apostle Paul was stuck in a Roman dungeon facing the possibility of execution at any moment. He had an excuse to be worried! Instead of worrying about dying, he prayed. He drew such strength from that practice that he wrote some letters to encourage worried Christians to do the same. Knowing the following words were

"Worry is wasting today's time to clutter up tomorrow's opportunities with yesterday's troubles."

inspired by God and penned by a man sitting in a damp, dark, depressing dungeon makes them that much more inspirational. "Don't fret or worry," he wrote in Philippians 4:6-7. "Instead of worrying, pray. Let petitions and praises shape your worry into prayers. Before you know it, a sense of God's wholeness, everything coming together for good, will come and settle you down" (*The Message*). When you face a challenging circumstance, you have two choices. You can lose heart and let worrisome thoughts control your mind; or you can pray about it. But you cannot do both simultaneously.

> "...A sense of God's wholeness, everything coming together for good, will come and settle you down."

I read about a Christian man who owned a construction company that was facing financial problems. One morning, after another sleepless night filled with worry, he opened his Bible and devotional guide and read Matthew 6 where Jesus commanded His followers not to worry. Jesus said, "Look at the birds of the air; they do not sow or reap or store away in barns, and yet your heavenly Father feeds them. Are you not much more valuable than they?" (6:26). A few days earlier at work, his crew had been clearing trees when he noticed a bird nest with baby birds inside one of the trees to be removed. He marked the tree and left word not to cut it down. However, as he closed his devotional book that morning, he realized the tree would have to come down that day because they couldn't delay the project any longer.

The owner used a bucket truck to lift him up to the bird's nest to see if the babies were still there. When he looked in, the birds were gone—they had fledged. Since he was up there anyway, he carefully removed the nest made with scraps of paper, twigs and bits of string. One sliver of paper was sticking out, so he pulled it and read the words printed on it. When he did, he almost fell out of the bucket! Written on the fragment were these words, "God cares for you." He realized God used that bird nest to reinforce His message. Today, the man's business is doing well; he prays more and worries less. And he keeps that bird's nest in his office!

Praying about what concerns you is not enough.

Pray Persistently

Praying about what concerns you is not enough. In the parable, the poor widow *kept* on begging the judge to grant her justice. She peppered his ears with persistent petitions. Have you ever asked God for something, and when He didn't answer your prayer immediately, you quit praying? You didn't P.U.S.H—Pray Until Something Happens. The people who prayed some of the most effective prayers in the Bible prayed persistently. God did not always answer them the first time. What makes us think He will answer our hasty, one-shot prayers?

In Psalm 55:16-17, David wrote: “I call to God, and the Lord saves me. Evening, morning, and noon I cry out in distress, and he hears my voice.” David wasn’t popping one-a-day vitamin prayers. He was an all-day, intravenous pray-er on a slow drip! In the Old Testament, Hannah desperately wanted a child and prayed for him or her many years to no avail. She didn’t give up. She kept on praying, and eventually God gave her a son named Samuel, the mighty prophet.

“I call to God, and the Lord saves me.”

Even Jesus prayed persistently. On the night before the crucifixion, He was in the Garden of Gethsemane pouring out His heart to His Father. His prayer burden was so intense that there were drops of blood-like sweat on His forehead. He prayed repeatedly for God to take away the “cup” of the task before Him if that was God’s will. Paul had an unidentified painful affliction he called a “thorn in the flesh.” He begged the Lord to remove it—not once, not twice, but three times. When God finally answered, it wasn’t the answer Paul wanted. God didn’t take away the thorn. Instead, He gave him the grace to cope with the pain. Persistence is a valuable commodity for every area of the Christian life, not just prayer. God blesses those who persist. If you're ever tempted to give up, just remember the composer Brahms. It took him seven long years to write his famous Lullaby (I guess because he kept falling asleep at the piano!).

One of the largest organizations in America is the Quitters Club. The reason you've never heard of the Quitters Club is because they never meet; the members quit coming. There are no dues; the members quit paying them. The Quitters Club is comprised of people who faced a tough job, a tough marriage, a tough sickness, or a tough failure—and they quit. However, God always honors persistence.

Persistence is a valuable commodity for every area of the Christian life, not just prayer.

Emmitt Smith set an NFL rushing record during his career. He wasn't as flashy as Walter Payton or Barry Sanders, and he never possessed true breakaway speed. His strength was in his ability to persist; he just kept on running no matter how many people tried to knock him down. When he set the record, he had run for 16,743 yards (about 9.5 miles). Think about that—it took him 13 years to run only 9.5 miles. I ran that much on the jogging trail last week. But I didn't have 11 huge defensive players trying to take my head off when I ran! Emmitt's average run over those 9.5 miles was 4.3 yards at a time. That means he had been tackled and knocked down 3983 times—and yet he got up and ran the ball again.

Even the best people get knocked down in life, but what sets them apart from the quitters is that they get right back up. You and I have an adversary who opposes us on every hand. The devil doesn't want you to P.U.S.H, and he'll do everything he can to make you stop praying! He has many weapons in his arsenal. He will use adversarial people who will tackle you and stomp on your dreams. If that doesn't work, difficult circumstances will trip your feet out from under you. The poor widow in Jesus' parable had been knocked flat, but she refused to stay down. She kept P.U.S.Hing.

> The devil doesn't want you to P.U.S.H., and he'll do everything he can to make you stop praying.

One of the greatest men of faith in Christian history was the English preacher, George Mueller. He wrote these words about praying: "The great point is never to give up until the answer comes. I have been praying for 63 years and 8 months for one man's conversion. He is not saved yet, but he will be. How can it be otherwise? I am praying." George Mueller eventually died, and the man was still not saved!

But as they lowered Mueller's casket into the

ground, the man for whom he'd prayed repented of his sins and trusted Jesus as his Savior. That was the result of persistent praying!

Pray Positively

So, if we are like the widow in this story, does that make God the crooked judge? Does He have to pestered and coerced before He will answer our prayers? Not at all. Parables not only contain comparisons but contrasts as well. Jesus used the mean judge as the antithesis of our loving Heavenly Father. He pointed to the ruthless judge in His story and said, "And will not God bring justice to His chosen? Will He not answer their prayers quickly?" Matthew 18:7 (NIV).

You *must* expect God to answer your prayers. If you doubt that you'll receive an answer, chances are you won't. In James 1, we learn that when we pray for wisdom God will give it to us generously. We ask; He gives. First John 5:14-15 adds, "This is the confidence we have in approaching God: that if we ask anything according to his will, he hears us. And if we know that he hears us—whatever we ask—we know that we have what we asked of him."

You *must* expect God to answer your prayers.

However, James also adds a powerful warning about letting doubt creep into your prayers when you ask.

He writes: "But when he asks, he must believe and not doubt, because he who doubts is like a wave of the sea, blown and tossed by the wind. That man should not think he will receive anything from the Lord" (James 1:6-7). Sadly, many Christians pray—and they pray persistently. Yet deep inside they really don't expect an answer. I heard about a Sunday school teacher who had her children write letters to a missionary for whom the class had been praying. Not wanting to disappoint the children if he didn't write back, the teacher explained that the missionary was very busy and wouldn't have time to reply to every child. One little boy then wrote this letter: "Dear Mr. Smith, I am praying for you. I am not expecting an answer." Can you relate? You pray, but are you expecting an answer?

> Sadly, many Christians pray... yet deep inside they really don't expect an answer.

When God Answers

Most people stop praying if they do not receive an answer from God right away. If I walk into a room and flip the light switch, I expect the light to come on. If it doesn't, I don't curse Thomas Edison and say electricity is founded on a lie. I start looking for the problem. Maybe the light bulb is burned out, or a breaker has been thrown, or the power is out. If it seems your prayers aren't answered, don't quit praying—

start looking for the reason why. *God always answers prayer.* But He answers our prayers in different ways.

QUICKLY

In the NIV translation, Jesus used the word *quickly* to describe how God answers prayer. *The Message* paraphrase says, "He will not drag his feet." The word "quickly" is a relative term though. If someone were injured, I would say, "Call 911 quickly!" However, if a couple gets married only four months after their first date, we might say, "They sure got married quickly!" A more accurate term for how God answers prayer is the word *suddenly*. Your prayers may seem to be unanswered for months and even years, and then BOOM!—one day God gives the answer.

God always answers prayer.

I heard about a lady who was rushing to the mall. It was pouring rain, and she didn't have an umbrella. As she drove into the parking lot she prayed, "Please, Lord, let me find a good parking place near the front door." Just as she said those words, she saw a car pull out of the best parking space in the entire lot. She put on her blinker and said, "Never mind, Lord, I found one myself!" God answered her prayer so quickly that she didn't even have time to understand it was God at work.

WAIT

God's delays are not His denials. Sometimes we must wait for our answer for a variety of reasons. Sometimes, the request is right, but the timing is not. From God's perspective, timing is always more important than time. And His timing is impeccable. Sometimes our request reflects an immature or selfish attitude. We must wait while God grows us spiritually so we can ask for and receive what He has in mind for us. Sometimes the delay is related to spiritual warfare. An example of this can be found in Daniel 10. Daniel prayed, and God dispatched the angel Gabriel to give Daniel His answer. However, the Prince of Persia (a demonic spirit) resisted Gabriel in delivering the message. The archangel Michael had to fight against the Prince of Persia so Daniel could receive God's answer. During the delay, Daniel modeled what we should do while we wait: he did not stop praying. If it seems God hasn't answered your prayer yet, don't quit! The answer could be just around the corner. So pray persistently, and then wait patiently for His answer.

> **If it seems God hasn't answered your prayer yet, don't quit!**

BETTER

Sometimes you don't get what you ask for because God has something better in store for you. Ruth Bell

Graham, the wife of Billy Graham, once said, "If God answered every prayer of mine, I would have married the wrong man seven times!" I had a friend growing up who had the ugliest bicycle I'd ever seen. It was a hand-me-down made from the parts of other bicycles. It didn't even have handlebar grips, and he was always complaining about his hands slipping off the slick steel posts. He pestered his dad to buy him some handlebar grips, but his dad refused.

One day, his dad took him to the Western Auto hardware store. Near the front door my friend saw some new handlebar grips for sale with long streamers hanging from the ends. He pleaded for his dad to buy them for him, but he just seemed to ignore his request. Sullen, he followed his dad to the back of the store, muttering aloud, "I never get anything I want. It's just a lousy three dollars! My dad sure is mean!" When they got to the back of the store, the owner wheeled out a shiny, brand new bicycle—complete with plastic streamers on the handlebars! His father wouldn't allow my friend to get the handlebar grips because he had something better in mind. Sometimes when you ask God for something good, He has something better in store for you!

> **Sometimes when you ask God for something good, He has something better in store for you!**

Maybe you've been praying a long time, and you have yet to receive anything "better." In fact, maybe you're discouraged because things seem to be getting worse; just wait. God always answers prayer in the way and at the time that will be for your greatest good and give Him the greatest glory. My late friend Ron Dunn wrote in his book, *Don't Just Stand There, Pray Something*: "God answers prayer along the route that brings Him the most glory. And on the way to better, it may pass by worse for awhile." So don't stop praying—even if things seem to be worse right now.

Sometimes you ask God for something, and His answer is simply, "No."

NO

Sometimes you ask God for something, and His answer is simply, "No." That's still an answer to prayer. Don't ever stop praying until you confirm that God has closed that option. At that point, stop making that request and start praying in a different way.

My mother lived with us when she was dying of cancer. I felt as if I did everything "right" in praying for her. I fasted, prayed and asked God to heal her completely. She did not get better. I prayed about it instead of worrying, and I prayed persistently. She seemed to get worse. I prayed in positive faith, fully expecting God to heal my mother. The reports from the doctor did not look good. After months of praying for God to heal her, one day He clearly spoke to my spirit and said, "David, I'm not going to heal her the way you want her healed. I'm going to totally heal her by bringing her home to be with Me." At that moment, I stopped praying for her healing.

But I didn't stop praying.

I changed my prayer to, "Dear Lord, keep her free from pain and help her to enjoy the days of physical life she has left." And God answered that prayer. C.S. Lewis wrote, "Prayer is request. The essence of a request, as distinct from a demand, is that it may or may not be granted. And if an infinitely wise Being listens to the requests of finite and foolish creatures, of course He will sometimes grant them and sometimes refuse them...If God had granted all the silly prayers I've made in my life, where should I be now?" I don't believe in "unanswered prayers," despite Garth Brooks' successful song with the same title. I believe God answers *every* prayer. He just doesn't *grant* every request.

I believe God answers *every* prayer. He just doesn't *grant* every request.

When People Pray

In 2002, the "Washington D.C. snipers" paralyzed millions of people with the fear that they would be their next victims in a random shooting. For three terrifying weeks, the authorities searched for them to no avail as our nation prayed and hoped they would be caught. We know the two men were arrested. They were caught at a rest stop when several people phoned 911 to report a car matching the description with the snipers sleeping inside. What you may not know is the backstory of how prayer led to their arrest. Ron Lantz, a trucker from Kentucky, was one of those at the rest stop who called 911 and then used his rig to block the exit ramp in case the suspects woke up before the authorities arrived. Ron never claimed to be a hero, but he did say that finding the snipers was an answer to prayer.

> "...A bunch of people praying together can be more powerful than a person praying alone."

A few nights earlier, he had joined over 50 truckers at a prayer meeting where they asked God to help them find the snipers. He later wrote in an article for *Guideposts:* "I got to thinking about what I'd learned at church, how a bunch of people praying together can be more powerful than a person praying alone. What if I get on my CB, see if a few drivers want to pull off the road with me and pray about this? I pressed the button on my microphone and said that if anyone wanted to pray about the sniper, he could meet me in half an hour at the eastbound 66-mile-marker rest area. A trucker answered right away. Then another and another. They'd be there. I hadn't gone five miles before a line of trucks formed, some coming up from behind, others up ahead slowing down to join us. The line stretched for miles" (Guideposts, "Prayer Convoy On Interstate 70," September 2003, pp.41-45). When we desperately need something to "happen" regarding our deepest concerns, we must P.U.S.H. in our prayers until we see God's hand move.

In Genesis 32, Jacob wrestled with an angel of God, wanting an answer to his request for God to bless him. They wrestled all night. Toward morning, Jacob had the angel in a full Nelson grip. I think it was more like the WWF wrestling show on television; it was a fixed fight. The mighty angel could have tossed Jacob off in a heartbeat, but God was teaching Jacob (and us) a valuable lesson about the power of persistent, tenacious praying. Remember, Jacob's name meant "grabber," since he was born holding onto the foot of his brother, Esau. Have you ever grabbed onto God in prayer and begged Him saying, "I'm not going to quit praying until you answer me?" Will you P.U.S.H that hard? Every time you walk through a door that says PUSH, let God remind you to Pray Until Something Happens!

We must P.U.S.H. in our prayers until we see God's hand move.

QUESTIONS TO THINK ABOUT

Who has taught you the most about prayer?

In what ways do you relate to the widow in this story?

Why should you pray if God knows what's going to happen anyway?

What are some different responses God gives to our prayers? Why doesn't He just grant us what we want?

What is your definition of persistence in prayer?

When was a time you refused to give up praying for someone or something? What was the result?

How would you like to grow in your prayer life six months from now?

CHAPTER 11

Grace: The Gift That Keeps on Forgiving

A Parable about Mercy

Matthew 18:23-35

In 1924, Victor Talking Machines trademarked the phrase: "The Gift that Keeps on Giving" to promote the sale of their talking machines, later called phonographs—long before the digital age of CDs and Mp3 players. By giving a phonograph as a gift, it would "keep on giving" enjoyment because the owners could listen to music for years. God's grace is the gift that keeps on for-giving.

We love to talk about how God has forgiven us, but we sometimes choke on the idea of forgiving others.

A pastor friend of mine tells the story of driving along as his two sons fought in the backseat. He looked in the rearview mirror just in time to see the foot of his ten-year-old connect squarely with the jaw of the seven-year-old, who started screaming in pain. The pastor pulled the car off the road, took his older son aside and demanded, "Why did you do that to your brother?"

"Because he keeps hitting me and won't stop."

Exasperated, the father said, "Son, why can't you just forgive him?"

As Christians, we're to turn the other cheek and forgive.

His son said, "Dad, why should I forgive him when I know he's going to keep on hitting me?"

My friend said that was a question he had often been asked by adults, and he still didn't have a good answer. The world's answer is simple—that's what payback is for. As Christians, we're to turn the other cheek and forgive. But sometimes forgiveness is very difficult when we know the person who needs our forgiveness most is going to "keep on hitting us." That's what Peter was saying when he asked Jesus how many times he had to forgive someone. Peter was looking for a number (he even suggested "seven" as a good round figure). Jesus told him it was a lot more than that—and then He told this story to prove His point:

The kingdom of God is like a king who decided to square accounts with his servants. As he got under way, one servant was brought before him who had run up a debt of a hundred thousand dollars. He couldn't pay up, so the king ordered the man, along with his wife, children, and goods, to be auctioned off at the slave market.

The poor wretch threw himself at the king's feet and begged, "Give me a chance and I'll pay it all back." Touched by his plea, the king let him off, erasing the debt.

Wow, isn't that a great story about forgiveness? Unfortunately, that isn't the end of the story. I wish it were. It would be much more pleasant than what actually happened next.

"The kingdom of God is like a king who decided to square accounts with his servants."

The servant was no sooner out of the room when he came upon one of his fellow servants who owed him ten dollars. He seized him by the throat and demanded, "Pay up. Now!"

The poor wretch threw himself down and begged, "Give me a chance and I'll pay it all back." But he wouldn't do it. He had him arrested and put in jail until the debt was paid. When the other servants saw this going on, they were outraged and brought a detailed report to the king.

The king summoned the man and said, "You evil servant! I forgave your entire debt when you begged me for mercy. Shouldn't you be compelled to be merciful to your fellow servant who asked for mercy?" The king was furious and put the screws to the man until he paid back his entire debt.

> And that's exactly what my Father in heaven is going to do to each one of you who doesn't forgive unconditionally anyone who asks for mercy. (***The Message,*** Matthew 18:23-35)

Peter's question demonstrated his attempt to be magnanimous. The Old Testament standard was retribution, not forgiveness. It was an eye-for-an-eye and a tooth-for-a-tooth society. However, the Jewish rabbis had long since adjusted that standard to say that a good Jew would forgive someone three times, but no more. For example, if a person stomped on your toe once, you should forgive him or her. If he or she stomped a second and third time, you might be mad, but still forgiveness was the right way to go. But a fourth time? Pow! Right in the kisser!

There should be no limits to forgiveness, as His story illustrates.

Peter offered to double that standard of three and add one for good measure. Jesus answered by saying that forgiveness isn't about keeping track; it's about building character. There should be no limits to forgiveness, as His story illustrates.

A Debt He Could Not Pay

In order to keep the characters straight, I often make up names in Jesus' parables. The king, of course, represents God. One day He will demand a full accounting for the debts all people owe Him as their Creator. The servant (we'll call him Hard-hearted Harry) owes an astronomical amount of money to the king. The word Jesus used could mean $100,000 or $10 million or $10 trillion because it was a word to describe an amount beyond belief. Harry fell on his knees and begged for mercy.

Harry owed the king a debt so large he could never repay it. Still, he arrogantly bartered for more time to pay him back. The king knew this was impossible, so Jesus said the king had pity on Harry. Jesus used a word that literally meant the king was moved with compassion. Did you notice that Harry got on his knees and begged, but he never said, "Forgive me for running up my debt"? It was the nature of the king to forgive, not to punish, so he offered the forgiveness for which Harry never asked. Knowing Harry's debt was impossible to pay off despite his supposedly good intentions, the king wrote the word "FORGIVEN" across the endless columns of numbers on Harry's audit scroll.

> **God offers us forgiveness because of His love for us, not because we have earned it.**

The only reason God offers us forgiveness is because of His love for us, not because we deserve it or have earned it. He offered forgiveness at Calvary before we even had enough sense to ask Him for it.

To get a handle on the enormity of Harry's debt, let's imagine you're a fairly righteous person and you only sin eight times a day. That's about one sin for every two hours you're awake. That's almost 3000 sins a year. If you started willfully sinning when you were about six years old and kept it up until age seventy-seven, that's a sum of over 200,000 sins. What if God rolled out a scroll with all 200,000 of those sins and said, "Here's your sin bill. What are you going to do about it?"

The Psalmist, equally humbled by the idea of a heavenly accounting of our sins, wrote in Psalm 130:3, "If you, O Lord, kept a record of sins, O Lord, who could stand?" Some may scoff at Harry for thinking he could pay off an insurmountable debt. However, that's very typical of human nature to try to fix our problem ourselves: *Lord, give me a chance. I'll clean up my act. I'll be nice to my family. I'll pay my taxes. I'll do ANYTHING!*

The cost of saving ourselves is far beyond what we can afford.

The cost of saving ourselves is far beyond what we can afford. The Bible says, "All have sinned and fall short of the glory of God and are justified freely by his grace through the redemption that came by Christ Jesus" (Romans 3:23-24). In the parable, writing off Harry's debt meant the king had to eat that debt himself.

When Jesus forgave our sin, He literally absorbed our debt into His body. That's why 1 Peter 2:24 says "He himself bore our sins in his body on the tree." Salvation is free to us, but it cost God the life of His precious Son.

Forgiving Others

So, the king erased Harry's debt, and they all lived happily ever after. If only we could have ended the story there! But Jesus often added uncomfortable twists in the plot of His parables. In the next scene, Harry leaves the king and happens across a fellow servant; we'll call him Debtor Dan. Hard-hearted Harry grabs poor Dan by the neck and demands that he pay him the $10 he owes. Dan reacts the same way that Harry did with the king. He fell to his knees and begged him saying, "Be patient with me and I'll pay you back."

Salvation is free to us, but it cost God the life of His precious Son.

To the surprise of everyone listening to Jesus' parable, Hard-hearted Harry refused and had Dan thrown into prison over a measly $10 debt. When word got back to the king about Harry's shenanigans, he was outraged. He summoned Harry to his courts and sentenced him to prison until he could pay off every cent he owed.

Some people misread this parable and think of it as transactional: IF I forgive others, then God will forgive me. That's not the case, even though the Bible does teach a relationship between acts of forgiveness. In the Sermon on the Mount, Jesus taught the disciples a model prayer in which we are to pray, "And forgive us our debts, as we also have forgiven our debtors" (Matthew 6:12). He also said in Matthew 6:15, "If you do not forgive men their sins, your Heavenly Father will not forgive your sins." But Jesus wasn't saying that we forgive others *so that* God will forgive us. That would be earning salvation through our own works. It helps to remember that the Sermon on the Mount is not telling lost people how to be saved; it is a code of conduct for everyone who is already a part of the Kingdom of God. It is written to people who have already been forgiven. You can argue about which came first: the chicken or the egg. However, you can't argue about which comes first—my forgiving others, or God's forgiving me. I forgive because God has first forgiven me.

> **I forgive because God has first forgiven me.**

Forgiveness is not an option for a true child of God. Paul writes, "Get rid of all bitterness, rage and anger, brawling and slander, along with every form of malice. Be kind and compassionate to one another, forgiving each other, just as in Christ God forgave you" (Ephesians 4:31-32). Harry's problem was the same one that many people still have. When it comes to us, we want grace; but when it comes to others, we want justice. Jesus warned those who claim to be forgiven but refuse to forgive others; they are deceiving themselves. Hard-hearted Harry doesn't represent a Christian who was once forgiven and then lost his salvation when he refused to forgive Dan. He represents someone who was offered unconditional forgiveness, but he refused to allow grace to change his heart. God cannot and will not forgive anyone who has a hard, unrepentant heart. How do we know the condition of our hearts? We reveal the true nature of our hearts by how we treat others.

We reveal the true nature of our hearts by how we treat others.

A Bitter Prison

Harry received a get-out-of-jail-free card, but when he saw Dan he refused to act from a position of grace. Instead, he said, "Go directly to jail. Do not pass go. Do not collect $200." In that moment of unforgiveness, Harry tore up his own get-out-jail-free-card. He sentenced himself to jail in that moment—long before the king imposed his sentence. Harry so wanted to punish Dan that he ended up punishing himself instead. That's what a spirit of bitterness and unforgiveness can do; it torments you instead of your enemy. Hebrews 12:15 says, "See to it that no one misses the grace of

God and that no bitter root grows up to cause trouble and defile many."

Warren Wiersbe comments of this parable: "The world's darkest prison is the prison of an unforgiving heart. When we refuse to forgive others we only imprison ourselves and compound our suffering. Some of the most miserable people I've met have been those who would not forgive others. They dream about punishing the one who wronged them, and don't realize that they are only punishing themselves" (*Meet Your King*, p.131).

> **The word *forgive* literally means, "to release."**

Pastor Ray Stedman once knew a sad woman suffering from bitterness. He wrote: "A woman in her eighties told me that, fifty years before, her aunt had said something insulting to her, and this woman had never forgiven her. Fifty years later she could recount the insult in precise detail, and as she talked about it, she felt all the same bitterness, anger, and resentment welling up within her as when it originally occurred. It was no wonder to me that, by this time, she had become a bitter, crotchety, quarrelsome, unhappy woman who could find no happiness in life whatsoever. She was still in the hands of the torturers fifty years later."

Throughout the years of being a pastor, many people have come to me for advice on how to forgive someone. They say, "Pastor, I WANT to forgive this person, I just don't know HOW." Some are troubled because they aren't sure if they have actually forgiven someone or not. I try to guide them by sharing three simple promises to make to someone when you forgive him or her. They are the same promises God makes to us when He forgives us.

When I forgive someone, I promise: I do not want to personally hurt you

The word *forgive* literally means, "to release." Harry physically grabbed Dan by the throat. Sometimes we do that mentally or emotionally with someone who has hurt us. When you forgive others, you release them from any personal desire you have to punish them. *What about someone who has committed a crime against me?* You can forgive that person and still allow the law to do its God-ordained job of punishing the evildoer. Surrender your right to be the police officer, judge, jury and executioner when someone hurts you. Release that person and the desire to exact revenge personally.

Sometimes we do that mentally or emotionally with someone who has hurt us.

When I forgive someone, I promise: I will not allow this incident to stand between us

True forgiveness wipes the slate clean so that a

broken relationship can be restored. That's what happens when God forgives us. Forgiveness is not the same thing as reconciliation. Forgiveness only requires one person to offer grace to another. Reconciliation requires two people (grace given and grace accepted). It's true of human relationships, and it's true of God. God unilaterally offers grace and forgiveness to everyone on this planet because He wants to be reconciled with every sinner. Does that mean everyone on the planet will accept His grace? Sadly, no.

God wants to be reconciled with every sinner.

In ideal scenarios, the offender asks forgiveness, and the offended person freely forgives. Then they reconcile their relationship. However, you don't have to wait for the offender to beg you for forgiveness before you extend grace. If you do, you may be waiting a long time. You can choose to forgive someone unilaterally apart from receiving an apology. Hopefully, the offender will accept your forgiveness and your relationship will be restored. Still, that might not happen either.

The Bible says, "If it is possible, as far as it depends on you, live at peace with everyone. Do not take revenge, my friends" (Romans 12:18). The Bible doesn't say you can live at peace with all people. You are only responsible for the part that "depends on you." Sadly, there are some people who cannot live at peace with others. They reject any and all sincere efforts you make at reconciling. What do you do then? Go ahead and forgive them anyway and move on. Forgiving does not make what they did to you okay; it makes you okay on the inside so you can experience peace.

When I forgive someone, I promise: I will not bring up the incident again

One husband told his friend, "When my wife and I argue, she gets historical." His friend said, "Do you mean hysterical?" The husband said, "No, she gets historical—she brings up all the mistakes I've ever made." When you forgive someone, resist the temptation to keep resurrecting the incident. Have you ever heard anyone say, "Well, I'll forgive you...but I won't forget about what you did"? Let me translate that for you: "I WON'T forgive you." Forgetfulness comes as a natural byproduct of getting older. Yet some people display a perfect memory when it comes to recalling how people mistreated or hurt them. Their emotions are just at the surface, and it doesn't take much for them to feel just as angry as when the original incident took place—even if it was decades ago. If it comes with conditions,

> "If it is possible, as far as it depends on you, live at peace with everyone."

it is not forgiveness. That's why Jesus concluded his story with the admonition to forgive "from the heart" (18:35, NIV) and "unconditionally" (The Message).

The Bible never says God forgets our sins. He's a lot older than us, but His memory is perfect. He is omniscient; He cannot forget anything. Instead, the Bible says He chooses not to remember our offenses. That's a big difference. God promises: "I am he who blots out your transgressions, for my own sake, and remembers your sin no more" (Isaiah 43:25). Realistically, you may never forget how someone offended you. Forgiving involves an active process where you make a conscious choice not to remember.

Realistically, you may never forget how someone offended you.

The great Baptist preacher from London, Charles Spurgeon, once wrote: "Forgive and let it go. When you bury a mad dog, don't leave his tail above the ground." That's what forgiveness is; you bury the deed in your subconscious and refuse to go digging for it.

If you ask Him, God can even help remove an insult or injury from your memory. Amy Carmichael, missionary to China, wrote: "If I say, 'Yes, I forgive, but I cannot forget,' as though the God who twice a day washes all the sands on all the shores of all the world could not wash such memories from my mind, then I know nothing of Calvary's love."

If only Harry had forgotten all about Dan's debt against him! Then he might have passed him by with a smile on the day he received such a tremendous gift of grace from the king. Harry would have come home to his wife and children and enjoyed a wonderful home-cooked meal instead of spending the first night of the rest of his life in prison.

An Alternate Ending

I like DVDs with special features added, including interviews with the director or, my favorite, outtakes. Some even contain alternate endings to the original movie. I envisioned an alternate ending to Jesus' parable after the king graciously absolved Harry of his debt and set him free. It goes like this:

If you ask Him, God can even help remove an insult or injury from your memory.

> When Harry went out from the king's courts, he ran into Debtor Dan, one of his fellow servants who owed him $10. At first, Dan averted his eyes and tried pretending he didn't see him. Harry was still relishing the freedom he'd just received two minutes ago and didn't even notice Dan in the hall. Harry had been losing sleep over the accumulating debt he owed the king, and now it was all forgiven. Suddenly, he felt Dan fall to his knees before him, begging, "Be patient with me, Hard-hearted Harry, and I will pay back what I owe you."

But Hard-hearted Harry was now Happy-hearted Harry. "Dan," he said to his fellow servant "what are you talking about?" (Before, Harry had been dwelling on the $10 Dan owed him since the day he borrowed it. Now, he couldn't even remember it.) He helped Dan to his feet. "But, but, but. . ." Dan began stuttering, convinced Harry was about to drag him before the king for punishment. "No buts. Whatever you may owe me is miniscule compared to my debt that the king just cancelled. I forgive you for not paying me back—don't worry about it."

Suddenly, Harry heard someone bellow his name down the long hallway. "Harry!" the voice shouted, "Come back in here." Harry and Dan didn't realize the king had been listening to their conversation outside the doorway. They exchanged worried glances. "You might need that $10 after all," Dan whispered. The king motioned for Harry to stand in front of him and said, "You faithful servant! Good for you! You canceled Dan's small debt just as I canceled your massive debt. Happy-hearted Harry, I hereby promote you to be my chief servant."

It's not too late to receive God's forgiveness and then keep on forgiving others from your heart.

And if the story had ended that way, Jesus would have said: "This is how my Heavenly Father will bless you if you forgive from your heart."

Are you sitting in the dungeon of an emotional prison of bitterness right now? Would you like an alternate ending to your situation? It's not too late to receive God's forgiveness and then keep on forgiving others from your heart.

QUESTIONS
TO THINK ABOUT

Why do you think Harry acted the way he did toward Dan?

Why do we often want mercy for ourselves and justice for others?

What is your definition of grace?

How can bitterness toward someone else actually end up harming us?

What do you do when you feel like holding a grudge?

What does it mean to forgive unconditionally?

What are you still learning about forgiving others unconditionally?